ROSES

To Rosie: who, until fairly recently, didn't like roses.

ROSES

Michael Marriott

CONTENTS

introduction

The romance of the rose

For thousands of years, roses have been valued for their beauty, perfume, and for their use in medicine. They often symbolize love, both human and spiritual.

Images of five-petaled flowers that could be roses can be seen on pottery shards found in the Jiangsu region of China dating back to 5000 BCE. They feature in Egyptian wall paintings and hieroglyphs from 2500 BCE, as well as in ancient Greek and Roman writings. The Greek scientist and philosopher Theophrastus, born around 371 BCE, wrote about the wild dog rose, as well as varieties with 12, 20, or even 100 petals. This gives us an early insight into roses' habit of readily mutating and crossing with one another to produce new variants—a natural consequence that occured once roses were transplanted from the wild into gardens.

Roses in Asia

Confucius (551–479 BCE) tells of roses being grown in the Imperial gardens in Beijing. Later, during the Han dynasty (206 BCE–220 CE), wild roses were grown on the palace walls. By the Tang dynasty (618–906 CE), the Chinese were known to be expert rose growers, and during the next dynasty, the Song, serious rose breeding began, before reaching its height during the Ming dynasty (1368–1644). The *Qun Fang Pu* (*Cyclopaedia of Flowers*) by Wang Xiangjin, published in 1621, mentions many of the 100 or so roses that were grown in China at that time.

While the category of "China rose" is well established (p.72), the names of individual Chinese varieties were actively disregarded by Western horticulturists when they brought these roses back to European markets. Thus, Mu Hsiang (Grove of Fragrance) became *Rosa banksiae*, while Yue Ji (Four Season Rose) was dubbed *Rosa chinensis*.

The Persian Prince Humay Meeting the Chinese Princess Humayun in a Garden
As its name suggests, this gouache artwork, painted in c.1450 and part of the Islamic School, depicts love at first sight in a rose garden.

In India during the 16th century, Emperor Shah Jahan was symbolized by a red rose, and there are many rose motifs on the walls of the Taj Mahal. The rose became known as a symbol for beauty: the Hindu god Vishnu is said to have created his bride, Lakshmi, from 108 large and 1,008 small rose petals. In southern India, the rose was central to the culture of both nobles and ordinary citizens of the Vijayanagara Empire (1336–1646). Abdur Razzak, a Persian diplomat, visited in 1443 and wrote, "Roses are sold everywhere. These people could not live without roses, and they look upon them as quite as necessary as food."

On the island of Java, in Indonesia, roses looking very much like 'Cramoisi Supérieur' and an unknown blush rose are grown on a large scale for the Muslim festival of Eid, in which people adorn the graves of their relatives with the blooms. The flowers are also used for other ceremonies and celebrations, such as weddings.

Roses in
Bud and Bloom
with Butterflies
and Insects
This artwork, part of the Chinese School, is thought to have been painted in the 18th century.

Roses in Europe

The Greeks and Romans used roses in their cooking and cosmetics, which means they must have grown them on a fairly large scale. But roses also played an important part in their ornamental gardens: Pliny the Younger, describing a garden in a letter, wrote, "a visitor on entering would look over the rose garden, whose scent would reach him." They used roses enthusiastically for their various festivals, celebrations, and banquets. The rose was associated with Venus (and, hence, with sex) as well as excess. At Cleopatra's first meeting with Mark Antony, a layer of roses a cubit (half a yard/meter) deep covered the floor and others hung from the ceiling in festoons. There is also the perhaps apocryphal story that at a banquet given by the third-century Roman emperor Heliogabalus, so many roses were dropped from the ceiling that some people drowned.

Over time, the rose transformed from a pagan symbol, with unsavory and decadent connotations in Greek and Roman life, to one that was central to both Christianity and Islam. It became a symbol for the Virgin Mary, who was described by the fifth-century poet Sedulius as the "rose among thorns." Perhaps the most obvious sign of the importance of the rose in Christianity are the magnificent rose windows in many churches and cathedrals. These are often dedicated to Mary, and she is depicted sitting in the middle. At Westminster Abbey an inscription on the floor says (in Latin), "As the rose is the flower of flowers, so is this the house of houses."

The allegorical *Roman de la Rose*, the story of a lover searching for his lady's love (the rose of the title), shows that in the 13th century the rose still stood for human (as well as spiritual) love. It describes a dream in which a lover is on a quest to pluck a rose, which he has seen on a rose bush reflected in the Fountain of Love at the center of a walled garden. The poem became one of the most influential and controversial works of the Middle Ages.

On a more practical level, a late 13th-century storekeeper's records, found in the debris of a perfume workshop in the Frankish castle at Pylos in the southwestern Peloponnese, show the trade in perfumed oils, including rose. This would have required the production of large numbers of blooms, and sophisticated equipment to produce the oil, and indicates how much rose perfume was valued.

The magic of scent

Most people's immediate reaction to seeing a rose is to
smell it. Even young children are drawn to smelling roses.
A deliciously fragrant rose has the wonderful ability to
both calm us down and raise our spirits.

Fragrances are generally strongest after a period of warm weather and immediately following some light rain, when the atmosphere is humid. They often develop and change as a flower opens, so it's important not to judge a variety's fragrance by a single bloom: if the flower is too young or too old, it is unlikely to smell of anything. Smell each variety on a regular basis: fragrances will often change dramatically from hour to hour, day to day, season to season, and even year to year.

The strongest fragrance is likely to be found when the bloom is at its most beautiful, but it's worth smelling two or three flowers at slightly different stages to find the best and to discover the differences between them. Don't rush in and give the flower a quick, embarrassed sniff. Smell it and smell it again, trying to gather as much fragrance from it as possible. It doesn't matter if you can't identify the scent: simply enjoy it for what it is.

Fragrance is a crucial part of why roses became so popular, perhaps due to the wonderfully strong and delicious perfume found in *Rosa gallica* and the other old roses. There are five main groups of fragrances, each originating from different rose types. Aside from tropical epiphytic orchids, no other plant has such a wide range of completely different fragrance types.

Old rose fragrance
This is the archetypal rose fragrance. There are subtle differences to be found between the different groups of old roses (pp.68–71): the gallicas have a richer, heavier scent, whereas albas are lighter and sweeter. When

found in more modern roses that have China roses in their parentage, like the Bourbons (p.73) and the English roses (p.82), a fruity element starts to appear.

Myrrh fragrance

The name is derived not from the biblical myrrh, but from the herb sweet cicely, *Myrrhis odorata*, which smells strongly of aniseed. This fragrance was found originally in the old rambler 'Splendens', descended from the white field rose, *Rosa arvensis*. From 'Splendens' came the pale pink gallica 'Belle Isis', which was one of the original parents that the British breeder David Austin used in his breeding program, specifically as a parent to his first variety, 'Constance Spry', which has a strong myrrh scent. It has since found its way into many other English roses. Some people dislike it, and it is true that in some varieties it is almost too strong, but it can be delicious, especially when it is combined with other fragrances.

Roses
This artwork is by Albert-Tibule Furcy de Lavault (1847–1915), who is known for his still-life paintings of cut garden flowers.

"Fragrance may be said to be the
other half of the beauty of a rose."
David Austin, *The English Roses*

Tea fragrance

Like the fresh tea leaves it's named after, this scent comes from China and
the Far East, originally from breeding the vigorous climbing species *Rosa
gigantea* with the bushy, repeat-flowering *R. chinensis*. It is found in more
modern varieties, especially in some hybrid musks and English roses,
but varies greatly, from a fresh violet fragrance to a harder, almost tarry
one. At its best, a superb fragrance.

Fruity fragrances

This covers a huge range of fruits, from apple, strawberry, raspberry, and
damson through all the different citruses to tropical fruits like mango,
guava, and lychee. These fragrances mostly come from two parents, *Rosa
chinensis* and *R. wichurana*, and are often combined with other scents,
especially old rose, to produce some truly delicious, almost mouthwatering
perfumes. Many of the English roses have fruity fragrances.

Musk fragrance

While all the fragrances described above come from petals, musk comes
from stamens and has the wonderful ability to waft on the air. It's particularly
common in ramblers, which also have great numbers of small single or
semi-double flowers and a large bunch of stamens in the middle. It is
reminiscent of the musk fragrance widely used in perfumes. At close
quarters, it often smells of cloves. Some varieties have just the right
combination of petals and stamens so that the musk can be appreciated
alongside the fragrance of the petals.

Leaves and "moss"

It is not just rose flowers that have attractive fragrances. The young leaves of
sweet briar, *Rosa rubiginosa*, have a delicious apple scent that is especially
noticeable on warm summer evenings. It can be kept clipped to encourage
as many young leaves as possible. The mossy growth around the buds of
moss roses and the glandular hairs around the buds of gallicas are quite
sticky and have an attractive, resinous smell.

The Soul of the Rose
This 1908 painting (also
known as *My Sweet
Rose*) by John William
Waterhouse is thought
to have been inspired by
Alfred, Lord Tennyson's
1855 poem *Maud*.

ROSE
inspiration

Rose gardens

A rose bed or garden offers the most intense rose experience. Roses can be used to carpet the ground, provide a backdrop, and arch over the paths.

The first recorded plan for a "rosarium" was drawn up in 1813 by landscape gardener Humphry Repton for Ashridge House in Hertfordshire, UK. It shows a number of coffin-shaped beds around a central fountain, set within a ring of rose-covered arches. At that time, though, there were few suitable roses for such a garden—proof, perhaps, that Repton didn't know his roses.

The development of hybrid-tea roses in the mid-19th century sparked the fashion for formal rose gardens. Like the floribundas that followed, these new roses had a long flowering season, so the gardens were colorful throughout the summer months and into the fall. The French were some of their greatest proponents, with the magnificent Roseraie de l'Haÿ and the rose garden in the Parc Bagatelle botanic garden in Paris, begun in the 1890s and in 1905, respectively.

This new fashion became so dominant that until the late 20th century, roses were mainly planted in formal rose gardens or rose beds. In private gardens, this could mean just a small circular bed, perhaps with a standard rose in the middle, or several beds set out in a symmetrical pattern. Every public park had a rose garden. Fungicides and pesticides were freely used to combat the pests and diseases that flourished in these monocultures. Later, as fashions changed (and gardeners learned to steer clear of toxic chemicals), the trend for mixed planting emerged (pp.24–33).

Planning a rose garden

While mixed plantings are beautiful, a well planted and maintained rose garden can still be superb. The beds need to be filled with roses, so that little or no soil is visible. This usually means planting them about 18in (50cm) apart, although larger varieties need more space, as do roses grown in warm climates. Individual beds can either be filled with one variety or, if space allows, a number of different ones. As far as colors go, the choices are wide, from pastel harmonies ('Queen of Sweden', 'Olivia Rose Austin', and 'Desdemona') to exuberant clashing kaleidoscopes ('Empereur Charles IV', 'Golden Beauty', and 'Lovely Parfuma').

Choose upright varieties so you can get between them in order to weed, dead-head, and so on. Since this is a monoculture, they also need a high level of disease resistance. Repeat-flowering and fragrance are usually prerequisites, too. This generally limits the choice to hybrid teas, floribundas, some English roses, and some Portlands.

A formal rose garden can be made to fit almost any space, the individual beds holding anything from just a few roses up to several hundred—as in Queen Mary's Gardens in Regent's Park, London, or Victoria State Rose Garden in Australia. It could be as simple as four beds surrounding a central

Roses in abundance
At the garden at David Austin Roses, Shropshire, UK, this tapestry of modern shrub roses is backed by paler climbing varieties and offset here and there by dark topiary pillars.

Modern formality
Every shade of pink rose, from
the palest bloom to a dark purple,
surrounds a formal fountain and
statue in a new rose garden in
Glyndebourne, Sussex, UK.

"Obelisks and pillars can add height to a border. They also provide winter interest, when the roses grown up them are bare of flowers and leaves."

Two tiers together
Tall standards of 'Ballerina' are grown above the same rose in its natural shrub form, fronted by lavender and a clipped low hedge.

circular bed or water feature, edged with a low hedge—perhaps yew, lavender, or *Euonymus* 'Jean Hugues'. Box is traditional, but is risky these days, due to box blight and box tree caterpillar, and its roots can seriously compete with those of the roses.

Adding height

Standard, or "tree," roses add an extra layer, either in the middle of the border or lining paths through the garden. They're sold with different stem lengths, to suit different positions. A full standard, with the flowers at about 4–5ft (1.2–1.5m), works well in most borders. Shorter stems can be useful for raised beds or containers, while weeping standards can make magnificent heaps of flowers. The stem itself is not very beautiful, so should be hidden by the other roses or plants around it. Standard roses need stout stakes to support their large heads. Sweet chestnut is particularly good for this purpose, as it will last 40 years in the soil with no preservative.

Varying the planting

Rather than sticking to similar-sized roses, for a more informal look you can combine rose types of very different heights and growth habits. How about planting the hummock-forming 'Flower Carpet White' next to the taller, more upright 'Champagne Moment', or the rounded 'Scarborough Fair' with the taller, shrubbier 'Princess Alexandra of Kent'? You might include some roses for their hips or colorful leaves (pp.158–63), although avoid any species roses that tend to spread by suckering, such as hybrids of *R. spinosissima*, as they may take over your border. You could also back your border with rose-covered walls, or add a pergola over the path through it.

As a halfway house to the mixed border, space your roses more widely and interplant them with low-growing perennials or bulbs. Some believe that aromatic plants such as alliums, lavender, or salvias keep roses healthier; and, of course, spring bulbs will brighten the bed before the roses start to flower. Do keep the area under each rose free of competition, though.

Mixing it up

Planting roses with perennials, biennials, annuals, bulbs, and other shrubs opens up endless possibilities for contrasting shapes and colors, and for creating atmospheric gardens.

Mixing roses with other plants may seem like a new gardening practice, but, in fact, there was great enthusiasm for this practice in the late 19th and early 20th centuries. In his best-selling 1883 book, *The English Flower Garden*, William Robinson railed against planting roses in rose gardens. He loved roses, writing that "the nobler flowers have been rejected as unfit for the flower garden [meaning the mixed border] in our day, and first among them the Rose." He goes on to say, "I begin the summer garden with the Rose, too long left out of her right place, and put in the background."

The mixed border has many advantages. It extends the flowering season, helps to keep the roses healthier, is a way of introducing blue into the color scheme and, perhaps most importantly, enhances the beauty of the roses by juxtaposing them with contrasting plants. Most shrub roses have an informal habit, matching that of most perennials, biennials, and annuals. The only roses that can be tricky to include in a mixed border are the more formal hybrid teas, floribundas, patio, and miniature roses, all of which are generally better suited to other places in the garden.

A 50:50 mix of roses and perennials works well, but there's no reason why you can't add just one rose, especially one full of character, like the beautiful rich-pink damask 'Ispahan' or the free-flowering apricot 'Lady of Shalott'. For more impact, if you have the space, plant three specimens close together (about two-thirds their width apart) to give the impression of one big bush.

Planning a mixed border

If you're making a new mixed bed, or taking over a neglected garden that you've cleared in order to start over, you can design your planting around roses. Use them to structure the site: as a backdrop on walls and fences, to provide focal points, and to grow beside paths or even over arches. Once you've figured out where your structural roses should go, add complementary perennials and bulbs around them—perhaps with annuals as gap-fillers in the first year.

The first thing to consider when planning to mix roses with other plants is how much space they need. With the exception of the tough species roses

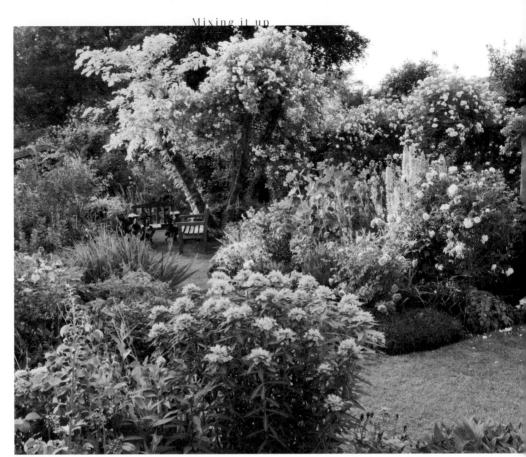

A mixed medley
Roses bloom throughout this colorful garden: shrub varieties bloom alongside euphorbia and delphiniums, a rambler grows through a tree, and the rear fence is clothed with climbing roses.

and their hybrids, roses don't like having other plants growing right around their base. Ideally, they should be planted far enough away that their outer edges just touch those of the rose, so that their flowers end up side-by-side. As a rough guide, add the suggested spreads for the rose and its proposed neighbor and then halve this total to determine the best planting spot. So, the planting hole for a 4ft- (1.2m-) wide rose needs to be about 3ft (90cm) away from that for a 2ft- (60cm-) wide perennial. They won't be mature, or probably in flower, when you plant them, and this distance can easily seem too great—but it is necessary, since perennials and biennials often have extensive root systems that will take the lion's share of water and nutrients from the ground, leaving little for the rose.

Annuals can be planted closer. They have a smaller root system that won't interfere with that of the rose. They often have a very long flowering season and can look lovely growing through roses. Try cosmos (pink, white, magenta, and even shades of yellow and orange), blue, white, or pink love-in-a-mist (*Nigella*), and orange to ivory marigolds (*Calendula*), which are fairly short, and so good in front of roses. One of the very best is *Phacelia tanacetifolia*, normally grown as a ground-cover plant. It grows

extremely easily from seed, flowers quickly, has pretty blue flowers and, importantly, is incredibly attractive to bees and other insects. It also seeds itself around with gay abandon, although it's easy to pull up should it get overenthusiastic.

Many perennials have the nasty habit of flopping over and resting on their neighbors, something young rose bushes do not appreciate. *Nepeta* (catmint) 'Six Hills Giant' is a classic example: it grows too tall and then collapses in strong winds or heavy rain, smothering its neighbors. To be safe, choose a shorter variety, like *N. x faassenii* 'Kit Cat'. Once roses are well established, a bit of gentle falling over (be it the rose or the perennial that leans) can look very pretty. Many of the gallicas have a fairly lax habit and can look beautiful with their flowers resting on their neighbors.

If you want to add some roses to an existing perennial border, beware of the illusionary gap. All too often, you'll identify an apparent space in a herbaceous border in winter or early spring, especially after pruning, and duly plant a rose in it. Perennials, though, are adept at filling spaces, and before too long the poor young rose will disappear under a tangle of stems. Make sure it is a real space in the border, and stake the perennials to stop them from flopping over, at least for the first year or two, until the rose can hold its own.

Combining plants

Roses are quite exceptional in having such a long flowering period. Most flower from late spring or early summer through to late fall or early winter. To extend this season even more, spring bulbs are an obvious addition. Many flower from late winter into spring, when roses are at their barest, having just been pruned. (You'll need to take care to leave room to get to your roses to prune them without trampling your spring bulbs, though.)

It is, though, when roses and their neighbors flower at the same time that magical combinations are created. It is easy to plant a range of roses and other plants and hope for the best, but the art of creating truly beautiful borders lies in identifying good partners that set each other off. This is the fun part of gardening: difficult to achieve, but so rewarding when it works. You'll need to think about not just the color, height, and shape of the plants, but also their character. How close a plant is to the original wild species will determine how formal or informal it appears. A big wild rose, for instance, will not go well with a highly bred *Echinacea* or *Antirrhinum*.

A living painting
In Yokohama English Garden, Japan, orange roses and rose hips mingle with the paler apricot shades behind, while the tall ornamental grasses, scarlet salvia, and silver-leafed tree provide depth and movement.

Try echoing the shapes of your roses: for example, you could interplant more upright roses, such as 'Queen of Sweden', 'The Lady Gardener', and 'James L. Austin', with foxgloves, delphiniums, and lupins—or contrast them with rounded plants like catmint, hardy geraniums, and herbaceous peonies. These might also hide the roses' bare legs, should they have them. Most shrub roses, though, have a more rounded, informal shape, so will contrast with tall, thin perennials or summer-flowering bulbs. Short, ground-hugging plants like Mexican fleabane (*Erigeron karvinskianus*), some hardy geraniums, and pinks (*Dianthus*) make perfect edging plants that fill the gap between the rose and the edge of the border.

Catching the sunlight
The bright pink blooms of 'John Clare' are here underplanted with lamb's ear and accompanied by Russian sage (right).

"When roses and their neighbors flower at the same time, magical combinations are created."

Consider flower size, too. Most roses have larger flowers than perennials, and you can choose plants that exaggerate this difference. For example, the large pink blooms of 'Olivia Rose Austin' look good next to catmint's small blue flowers. Later in the season, the myriad small flowers of *Symphyotrichum* (formerly *Aster*) 'Little Carlow' contrast beautifully with the wide, warm-pink, open flowers of 'Eustacia Vye'. The reverse is possible, too: the small-flowered, purple-pink rose 'Sibelius' with blowsy, pale-pink peony 'Sarah Bernhardt' or white 'Matchball' backed by hollyhocks.

The next consideration is height. To create the best color combination, the blooms of the plants you're combining should end up close to each other, and, in general, taller plants work best behind shorter ones, especially if the border is being viewed just from one side; for example, if it's backed by a wall, fence, or hedge. But this shouldn't be made an absolute rule: it would be dull indeed if everything were in serried ranks, in strict height order from front to back. Height variation within the border will liven it up, and any rose with a good fragrance should be easily accessible for regular sniffing. Sometimes it is effective to look through a light, airy plant like the grass *Stipa gigantea* or the ornamental thistle *Cirsium rivulare* 'Atropurpureum' to the rose behind it.

The rather stiff, upright growth and brightly colored, stylized flowers of most hybrid teas mean that they tend to clash with the traditional companions for roses, which mostly have small, softly colored flowers and a relaxed growth habit. While perhaps not to everyone's taste, a mixture of brightly colored hybrid teas, floribundas (such as 'Golden Beauty', 'Fruity Parfuma', and 'Natasha Richardson'), and similarly vivid, upright companions could be fun—perhaps in a tropical-style garden.

There are some more informal, graceful hybrid-teas with scented single flowers, such as apricot 'Mrs. Oakley Fisher' and pink 'Dainty Bess', and others with flowers very much in the style of old roses, such as creamy-yellow 'Concorde' and soft-pink 'Amorosa'. All of these are much easier to weave into a mixed border. The floribundas offer more exceptions: white or pastel varieties like 'Iceberg' and 'Champagne Moment' associate easily with other plants, while 'Lovely Parfuma' and 'Caroline's Heart' both have pink flowers and would fit in well.

A rich combination The changing colors of *Rosa* x *odorata* 'Mutabilis' work well with the mysterious, rather dark heads of *Allium sphaerocephalon*.

Color effects

While it is, of course, possible to plant with no thought of color association and end up in a glorious jumble, it's worth editing your palette down to find the best color companions. You could combine shades that are close to each other, such as yellow and apricot, or opposites like yellow and purple. Fewer colors work especially well in small spaces.

Use intense colors if you want to create a powerful and exciting effect (although if you get the shades wrong, your mistake will be obvious): magenta 'Empereur Charles IV' with the late-flowering *Aster* x *frikartii* 'Mönch', or purple 'Sibelius' with a dark lupin such as 'Masterpiece'. Soft shades are much easier to combine: even if they are not ideal companions, the clash will not be so glaring. Try white 'Summer Memories' with one of the pale geraniums like mauve *G. renardii* or white *G. macrorrhizum* 'White-Ness', 'Eustacia Vye' with the pale pink *Astrantia* 'Buckland', or soft apricot 'Stéphanie d'Ursel' with the yellow, fragrant daylily *Hemerocallis* 'Lemon Bells'. If you feel a border of nothing but soft shades might look rather dull, use a stronger color to add some lively focal points.

Soft contrasts
The blue hardy
geranium sets
off the soft pale
colors of 'Emily
Brontë' and white
foxglove in this
mixed bed.

"It's worth editing your palette
down to find the best color
companions: neighboring shades
like pinks and purples work well."

While it's all very well talking about how to create the perfect color association, in practice it is difficult to do so accurately from pictures and descriptions. If you can, cut a flower from the rose you're trying to place and walk around your garden or your local nursery, offering it up to other plants. This will give you a much better insight into the best combinations. Some will not work at all, others will look all right, and some will really spark off each other.

It's important to take account of all the different stages of a rose flower. The bud is often a very different color from the open flower, which may change dramatically again as it fades. Stand back to get an overall impression of the plant—you could seriously upset your carefully planned color scheme if you get distracted by the stage (often the bud or new flower) that attracts you most.

Reinventing the shrubbery

A shrubbery has a rather old-fashioned, Victorian ring to it, conjuring up an image of an overgrown, gloomy, neglected corner. Instead, why not choose tall roses and other flowering shrubs to create a colorful, fragrance-filled spot with year-round interest? Some long-flowering, mostly tall, roses that would work here are soft yellow to pink *R. x odorata* 'Mutabilis', 'Clair Matin', deep-pink 'Vanity', and pink-and-white 'Ballerina'; 'The Lark Ascending', 'Buttercup', 'Tottering-by-Gently', 'Morning Mist', and 'Penelope' also have hips.

Witch hazel (*Hamamelis*) would add winter flowers; acers and berberis good fall leaf-color; spindle, berberis and skimmia winter berries. Buddleia, hydrangea, philadelphus, skimmia, and lavender would give extra flowers to complement the roses.

Precious jewels
Here, 'Gertrude Jekyll' is set off by sapphire delphiniums and *Salvia nemorosa* 'Amethyst' to create a rich assortment of complementary jewel tones.

Rose hedges

Whether planted with a single variety or several, a rose hedge can be magnificent. Or, inspired by wild hedgerows, you can make a mixed hedge of roses and other shrubs.

Roses can make a colorful, impenetrable boundary or a low, fragrant internal divider. Substantial, wilder, thorny varieties, ones that don't necessarily repeat-flower but will set hips in the fall, are a good choice for external boundaries. The classic is *Rosa rugosa* and its hybrids (p.163); they are particularly tough and healthy, flower over a long period, and many produce cherry-tomato-sized hips. Other species roses and their near hybrids, or some of the more modern, small-flowered hybrid musklike roses (such as 'Sweet Siluetta' and 'Grand-Duc Jean', with carmine-red flowers and a white eye), would also be excellent.

For an internal barrier, the best choice is a more upright, compact, and less thorny rose, ideally one with a good fragrance. Many English roses and floribundas, such as 'Queen of Sweden', 'The Lady Gardener', and 'Île de Fleurs' work well.

Blooming boundary
This hedge of the shrub rose 'Sea Foam' forms part of a large-scale landscaping project across the town of Aurora, New York.

Bold choices
The vivid
orange shades of
'Lady of Shalott'
make for an
eye-catching hedge
in the garden at
David Austin Roses,
Shropshire, UK.

Since you are planting a row of roses—often of the same variety—quite closely together, it's important to choose ones with excellent disease resistance. As for spacing, an easy rule of thumb is to plant them half their width apart, so roughly 1½ft (50cm) apart for a rose that grows 3ft (1m) wide. They could go closer if you want to make a dense hedge quickly, or farther apart if you're aiming for an airy, see-though screen.

For an informal look, combine roses of different heights and widths, or mix them with other shrubs, as happens naturally with wild roses. You could stick to species roses, mixed with honeysuckle, field maple, blackthorn and hawthorn, or use longer-flowering garden varieties that have a wild feel to them, such as 'Île de Fleurs' or 'Goldspatz', *Lonicera periclymenum* 'Scentsation', *Lonicera* x *purpusii* 'Winter Beauty', and a small crab apple— 'Evereste', for example, can be pruned as a hedge.

Growing up & over

Roses are surely the best of all climbing plants. They are wonderfully variable and versatile, many are long-flowering and scented, and there is one to fit just about any vertical surface in the garden.

It is important to choose the right-sized variety for the position you want to grow it in. An overly vigorous rose will become a menace if grown up a small support. A correctly sized variety might take longer to mature, but it will then be easy to maintain, flower more freely, and generally look right.

Covering walls & fences

Of all the places it is possible to grow roses, training them up the wall of a house, especially on either side of the front door, must be one of the most common. Climbers are usually the best choice, as all but the shortest ramblers can be too vigorous and hard to manage on walls. Choose a variety with as long a flowering period as possible, or else extend the season of interest of a once-flowering rose by growing another climber, such as a clematis, through it.

The color of the rose's flower needs to work with the color of the wall. A warm pink or white usually goes with red brick, but it's safest to hold a flower up against the wall to see if it works. Painted walls and fences are easier, but it is still important to consider color: a pale rose on a pale background won't create much of an impact. Instead, how about a deep pink or purple rose—'Gertrude Jekyll' or 'Purple Skyliner'—for a white or cream wall, or yellow or apricot—'Golden Gate', 'Ghislaine de Féligonde', or 'Lady of Shalott'—against a soft yellow wall? And don't forget that unpainted fences are liable to fade to gray as they age.

For a 6ft (2m) fence, look at climbers up to 10ft (3m) tall (they'll be fanned out against the fence) or the larger shrub varieties, which will easily grow to that height, especially against a warm fence or wall. Tying the stems to screws or wires attached to vine eyes is the easiest way to support them (p.238).

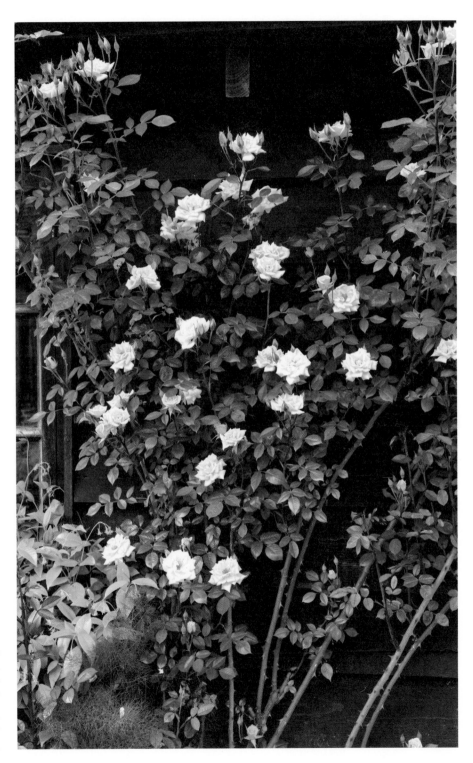

Creating contrast
A dark wall provides the perfect backdrop for the bright, creamy-yellow blooms of 'Laura Ford'.

A charming climber
Clothing this stone wall is the climber 'Mary Wallace', making an eye-catching display in Les Jardins de Roquelin, a rose garden in the Loire Valley, France.

Arches

Arches work best when they serve a clear function in a garden: for instance, by marking the transition from one area to the next. They can be made out of wood or metal and can be rustic, minimalist, or highly ornamental in style (although any ornamentation may well be hidden by the rose).

Metal arches don't rot and are available in a variety of finishes; powder-coated colors should last a long time. Wooden ones tend to have a limited life span, especially if the base is sunk in the ground rather than into a metal post base. Sweet chestnut, though, will last 40 years in the ground with no preservative. Whatever the material, an arch needs to be substantial to take the weight of the roses covering it, especially on a windy day. It needs to be at least 8ft (2.5m) high and 6ft (2m) wide, or it will be difficult to walk through without being attacked by the roses growing over it.

Choose varieties whose growth is relatively lax, or else they will send up vertical canes at the top that will look unattractive and be difficult to tie down. Many of the climbing English roses, as well as the patio climbers and ramblers, are particularly well-suited to arches, since they have the natural ability to flower more or less from the ground up—for example, 'Rambling Rosie' and 'Scent from Heaven'.

Blooming walkway
In Butchart Gardens, Victoria (British Colombia, Canada), a series of rose-covered arches creates a vibrant walkway for visitors to enjoy.

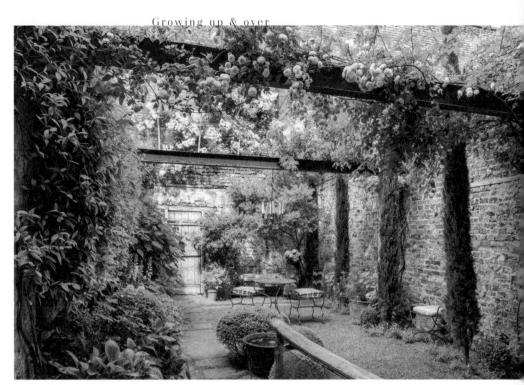

Urban greenery
In this courtyard garden, 'Rambling Rector' blooms across steel girders, making the most of the light in this semi-shady space.

Pergolas

A pergola is effectively a series of joined-up arches that form an airy tunnel. It can be made entirely of wood, or more permanently by building brick or stone pillars and bridging them with horizontal wood beams. As with arches, the pergola needs to be high and wide enough that the roses don't obstruct the way through. And it is even more important that roses chosen to grow over a pergola have lax stems so that they can be easily trained horizontally: this generally means the ramblers. As most of these do not repeat-flower, a possible solution is to plant both a climber and a rambler at the base of each pillar: the former to clothe the vertical section and keep flowering later in the season, and the latter to grow up and over the top, its blooms hanging down gracefully. To encourage flowers right from the base of the pillar, circle the stems around the uprights at an angle of about 45 degrees.

Obelisks & pillars

Obelisks are useful for creating structure and adding height to a border. They also look good in winter, when the roses growing up them are bare of flowers and leaves. They come in a wide range of shapes and sizes and it's particularly important to consider the height you'll need for your garden. If too short, the obelisk will be lost among the other plants growing around it. If too tall, it will dominate the border.

Obelisks are neat, geometrical shapes, and to show them off at their best, anything grown up them needs to look in scale and not too out of control. This means that some of the more upright, taller shrubs, such as 'The Lady Gardener', 'Summer Memories', and 'The Ancient Mariner', are good options, rather than climbers or ramblers. To encourage as many flowers as possible and help limit the rose's height, circle its stems around the structure. Avoid choosing an overly vigorous rose: it's likely to overwhelm the obelisk and then look untidy.

Like obelisks, pillars can add height to a border, but they take up less space at ground level. Since they are usually no more than 4–6in (10–15cm) wide, circling a rose's stems around them is not easy. But, by spacing three or four pillars 8–12in (20–30cm) apart in a triangle or square, you can create more of a statement and make it easier to encircle the structure with roses. Pillars need roses of a suitable height that can be kept neat. Some of the shorter climbing and rambling English roses, as well as patio climbers and ramblers, will be good choices: for example, 'Lady of the Lake', 'Open Arms', and 'Rambling Rosie'.

Growing through trees

A rose-covered tree is a splendid sight, with flowers hanging down in large, fragrant garlands, and with the right choice, masses of small orange or red hips. Ramblers are usually a better choice than climbers, as they are more likely to be able to compete successfully with the tree, and their lax growth will hang down more gracefully. Thorns come into their own in this situation, being the mechanism by which roses hang onto branches. While a thornless rambler might sound attractive, it is more likely to be blown out by the wind. The greater the number of thorns, and the more recurved they are, the better the rose will hang on.

It is important to match the vigor of the rose to the size of the tree: a super vigorous 26ft (8m) rambler such as 'Climbing Cécile Brunner' will be absolutely superb in a large tree like an oak or beech, but will quickly smother and kill a small or even medium-sized tree. The tree will eventually fall over, creating a magnificent rose heap—but this is only practical if you have a considerable amount of space.

For a medium-sized tree—say a birch, hazel, or an old apple—moderately vigorous ramblers like 'Adélaïde d'Orléans' and 'Francis E. Lester', which grow to about 16ft (5m), work well, allowing some of the supporting tree to show through. For a small tree like a hawthorn or a

"Ramblers are excellent for growing through trees: their flowers will hang down from branches in festoons."

cherry, varieties that grow only 6–13ft (2–4m) tall, such as pink 'Debutante' or 'Paul Noël' are perfect; the latter is also repeat-flowering, which is rare in ramblers.

Climbing companions

Rambling and climbing roses make wonderful supports for other climbers. There is a huge range of potential companions available in every conceivable size, but while a small climber can be grown up a large rose, the reverse (a *Clematis montana*, for example, growing up a 10ft (3m) climbing rose) would result in the rose being smothered.

The main choice is between using other climbers to extend the rose's season of interest (especially if, like most ramblers, it has just one glorious display in early summer) or going for planting partners whose flowers enhance each other. Clematis are perhaps the best climbers for

Clothing branches with blooms
In Yokohama Rose Garden, Japan, the large-flowering Pierre de Ronsard climbs up a tree, surrounded by a host of other varieties including Princess Alexandra of Kent, *R.* 'Sakurajima', *R.* 'Hiroshima-no-Kane', and *R.* 'Pēnelopeia'.

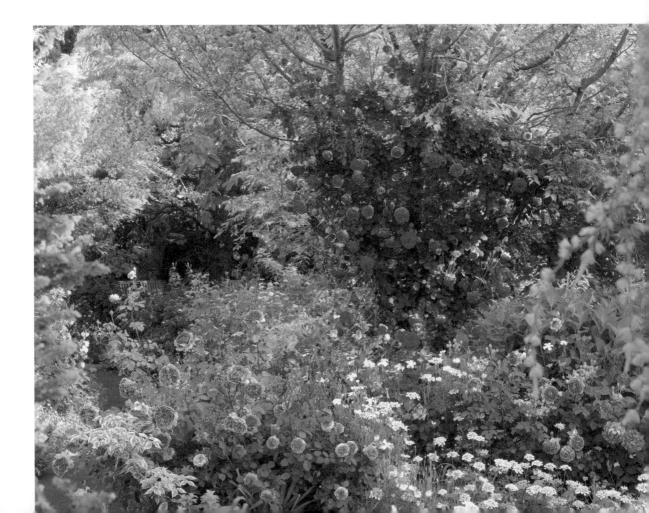

this purpose. They come in all different shapes and sizes, and it is possible to find one that flowers in every season, as well as a number that reliably repeat-flower over many months. 'Shimmer' is mid-purple to blue and grows to about 6ft (2m); 'Rebecca' grows to 8ft (2.5m) and has red flowers. Both flower from May to September. The late-flowering *Clematis viticella* varieties are always good with roses—for example, purple-pink 'Abundance', deep purple 'Black Prince', and white 'Alba Luxurians', which all grow to 10–13ft (3–4m).

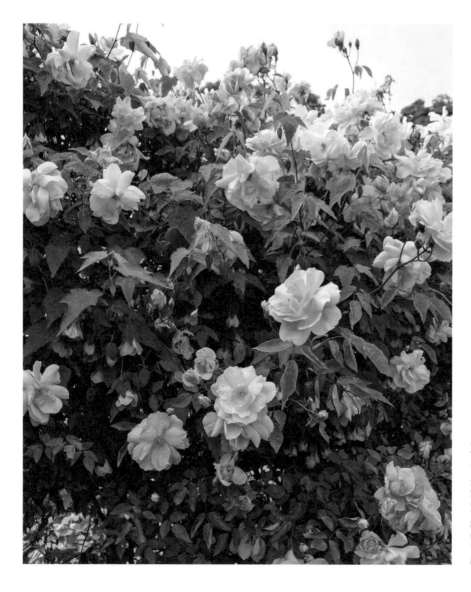

Apricot delight
The climbing rose 'Crépuscule', with its apricot-yellow blooms, mingles here with the rich gold and plum shades of abutilon 'Orange Hot Lava' (California).

> "Enhance the beauty of your roses by juxtaposing them with contrasting plants."

For spring interest, the *Clematis macropetala* hybrids flower April to May and grow to about 10ft (3m)—for example, white 'Albina Plena' or violet 'Octopus'. Blue *Clematis alpina* 'Pamela Jackman' flowers a little earlier, from March to April. *Clematis rehderiana* and *C. tangutica* and its hybrids are more vigorous and have yellow flowers from July to October. They look good growing up a rambler rose and have attractive seed heads.

Clematis do have an extensive root system which, when mature, will compete with that of the rose, so it may well be best to let the rose get established for two or three years before adding a clematis, or else planting it at least 3ft (1m) away.

Honeysuckles are another wonderful group of climbers, but many are so vigorous that they will easily smother a smaller rose. Some of the smaller ones are creamy-yellow *Lonicera etrusca* 'Superba', red *L. x brownii* 'Dropmore Scarlet', and *L. periclymenum* 'Scentsation', all of which will flower around the same time as roses.

In mild areas with light frosts, *Sollya heterophylla*, with its small bright-blue flowers would be effective. *Jasminum officinale* 'Devon Cream' or one of the star jasmines (*Trachelospermum* hybrids) add starry cream or white flowers and sweet perfume. Passionflower will twine through larger roses enthusiastically, adding an exotic touch.

Annual climbers can work really well with roses, as their root systems aren't as competitive as those of perennial ones. They also tend to have a longer flowering season. All can be grown from seed or are available as young plants in the spring. Purple *Cobaea scandens* (cup-and-saucer vine) flowers until the end of fall and looks good next to other deep colors, such as rich apricot 'Lady of Shallot' or crimson 'Climbing Étoile de Hollande'.

Ipomoea purpurea (morning glory) has trumpet-shaped blue, red, pink, or purple flowers, which look dramatic twining through a bright-pink rose like 'Gertrude Jekyll'. *Lathyrus odoratus* (sweet pea) is good, especially the old variety 'Cupani', which has the most superb fragrance. Its maroon and purple is an intriguing and vivid partner for the apricot and rose-pink of *Rosa x odorata* 'Mutabilis'. Sweet peas like plenty of moisture, so an occasional good soaking will help with their flowering.

For really tropical colors—perhaps to back some bright hybrid teas—*Thunbergia alata* (black-eyed Susan) has orange flowers with dark brown centers; there are varieties in other colors ranging from pink through yellow to cream.

Roses for fall & winter

Long-flowering varieties, those with colorful fall leaves and hips, and ornamental training of ramblers all offer interest during the dark months of the year.

The great majority of roses grown in gardens today will repeat-flower and, compared to most other plants, have an extremely long flowering season. They usually start up in early summer and, in temperate areas, finish in late fall or early winter. Some though, with decent weather and a sheltered position, will carry on up to Christmas—and, indeed, may never stop. The tea roses are the main group to do this, although they do require a warm climate year-round to flourish. The Chinas, too (especially *Rosa* × *odorata* 'Bengal Crimson' and 'Mutabilis') will carry on and on, and are not quite so fussy about it being warm the rest of the year. In climates whose "winter" is equivalent to a temperate season's summer, most repeat-flowering roses will produce their best flowers at that time, before taking their rest during the hot summer.

Some varieties have excellent fall leaf-color, notably *R. spinosissima* 'Grandiflora', *R. virginiana*, *R. nitida*, and *R. setigera*. *Rosa rugosa* leaves turn soft yellow, although only briefly, before they drop.

Frosty elegance
In the grounds of Dunrobin Castle, Scotland, the near-bare stems of these climbing roses make an arresting winter sight across pyramid frames.

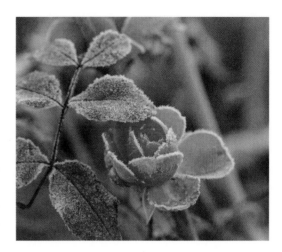

Winter beauty
As temperatures
fall, the long-
lasting blooms of
'Bonica' may be
touched by frost.

Hips can provide winter color (pp.158–163), as long as you choose those that last. Those on *Rosa sericea*, for example, drop quickly after coloring up. *Rosa rugosa* hips and some of the Chinese species like *R. moyesii* and *R. sweginzowii* look attractive until early winter, while others still look good well beyond midwinter. Because it's generally assumed that roses should be dead-headed, potential hip production is not recorded for many varieties. It's worth leaving the spent blooms on some to see what happens.

Mix hip-bearing roses with other shrubs with good fall color or berries, such as *Cornus sanguinea* 'Midwinter Fire', *Aucuba japonica* 'Crotonifolia', or *Skimmia japonica* 'Nymans'. Adding winter-flowerers like *Edgeworthia chrysantha*, *Lonicera fragrantissima*, or *Corylopsis pauciflora* will carry the interest through to the following spring.

The more vigorous ramblers can be trained in an ornamental way so that they look attractive between pruning and leafing out. Rather than cutting their long, flexible stems back, they are wound around in circles; this has the added advantage of encouraging more flowers. Climbers tend to be too stiff for this, and they also resent having their stems facing downward.

Tricky sites for roses

Not all gardens offer ideal conditions for roses, due to lack of space, poor or no soil, extreme temperatures, or shade, but there are ways to work around these problems.

Poor soil

Most roses prefer a reasonably good, well-drained soil, although many will still grow well in less-than-ideal conditions with the addition of well-rotted organic matter (pp.224–25). If your soil is particularly shallow or fast-draining, it's worth trying tough varieties such as 'Bonica', *Rosa* × *alba* 'Alba Semiplena', or *Rosa* × *richardii*. On really sandy soils, species roses that grow wild along the coast, like *Rosa rugosa* and *R. spinosissima*, are the best choice. Their respective hybrids will do well, too, as long as they are on their own roots or planted deeply enough to encourage rooting from the base of the stems.

While roses like a moist soil, the great majority will not grow well if their roots are wet for too long. The American species *Rosa palustris* and *R. californica*, both with rich-pink single flowers, are exceptions, having evolved to grow well in saturated soil. *R. virginiana* also flourishes in fairly wet soils, even those on the edge of salt marshes.

Using containers

If you can't plant them in good soil, you can grow roses successfully in large containers (pp.227–28). Terra-cotta or glazed pots offer better insulation for the roots than plastic, but you may still need to move the pots into a sheltered spot or wrap them in burlap or bubble wrap if the temperature drops below −5°F (15°C), since plants in pots are more vulnerable than those in the ground.

Being raised up, with no competition or shading from the side, any rose grown in a container is likely to bush out sideways and create a more rounded shape. Still, it's best to start with a compact variety that has a fairly bushy habit, like 'Desdemona' or 'Fruity Parfuma', otherwise the upright stems will be very evident. Repeat-flowering and fragrance are desirable, if not essential, requirements. Good disease-resistance is important, since the limited space of a pot can be quite stressful for the plant and make it more susceptible to diseases (although the greater airflow will help to ward them off). Many of the English roses are ideal, as are the floribundas (although fragrance is not their strong point). The smaller roses—miniatures, patios, and polyanthas—are also potential candidates, although fragrance is lacking in many of them. See pp.118–123 for more recommendations.

It's possible to grow shorter climbers and ramblers like 'Rambling Rosie' or 'Open Arms' in containers, and so be able to cover walls and fences. Some of the shorter "half" or "quarter" standard roses also work well, preferably with other plants such as *Erigeron karvinskianus* (Mexican fleabane) around their base.

Growing a rose in a pot makes it into a focal point, especially if it's a small variety that might otherwise get lost in a mixed bed. It's fun to group other pots around it and experiment with different planting combinations. You can swap these around seasonally: for example, winter foliage plants such as *Bergenia purpurascens* var. *delavayi* or heuchera, followed by spring bulbs, and then summer perennials or bedding. In a really large container, you could even underplant the rose, perhaps with aubretia or *Phlox subulata* to trail over the edge.

Extreme temperatures

Gardens in some parts of North America enjoy a temperate climate, where summers are rarely baking hot and winters are usually fairly mild. If you have a sunny coastal or urban garden, you will probably succeed with tea roses and be able to enjoy year-round flowers from Chinas. In places with really hot, dry summers, wild roses from places with a similar climate will thrive, such as the Mediterranean *R. gallica* and the Chinese *R. hugonis*.

Tolerance to winter cold differs greatly between varieties. Some, like the rugosas and other species native to northern areas, can withstand extreme cold down to USDA Zone 2. The great majority of garden roses are fine with winters in USDA Zone 7, with a number able to survive USDA Zone 5.

Sharp drops in temperature, alternating with warm periods in late winter or early spring, are potentially damaging. If such cold spells are forecast, roses can be protected by leaning conifer branches against them. In more extreme conditions, wrapping burlap or piling up soil, straw, or leaves around the stems works well. Roses in containers are particularly susceptible to the cold, but can be brought inside an unheated garage or shed for the winter.

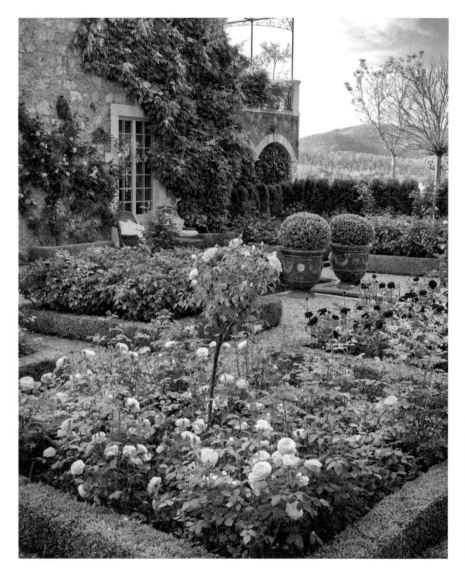

Tuscan sunshine
The Rose Garden at Borgo Santo Pietro, Italy, includes the white blooms of 'Winchester Cathedral' alongside the dark red roses of 'The Prince', with each bed framed with low box hedging.

Shady spots

When certain roses are recommended for shade, this does not mean that they will cope with no direct sunlight at all. Rather, these are varieties that need as little as four hours of direct sun a day—what most gardeners would consider "semi-shade" rather than shade. However, this does open up many more planting possibilities, especially in small city gardens that are inevitably shaded for part of the day by surrounding buildings or trees, and where close planting means plants tend to shade each other. Roses can even be grown successfully against north-facing fences or walls, as long as they are not also shaded from the east or west.

As a general rule, once-flowering varieties like 'Alba Maxima', 'Ispahan', and 'Celsiana' cope better with shade than those that repeat-flower. Nevertheless, many of the latter will be fine, although because their leaves may stay wet for longer, disease may be more of an issue so it is important to choose varieties that are naturally very healthy, such as 'Olivia Rose Austin' and 'Joie de Vivre'.

Any variety that tends to send out long shoots may get drawn toward the light and be less successful in a shady spot. Sturdier, bushier varieties like 'Kew Gardens' and 'Bonica' will generally be better, especially if you want to grow roses under trees. A rambler, on the other hand, will be drawn up through the tree and eventually reach the sun.

Layers of interest
Featuring roses including 'Felicia', 'Munstead Wood', and 'Gertrude Jekyll', this mixed border is staggered across a series of stone walls to create height.

Inspired by nature

Many modern roses, as well as the species from which they are bred, have a wild feel to them and make great features in naturalistic planting plans.

Wild gardens

Think of a romantic, overgrown cottage garden that mixes roses with old favorites such as peonies, delphiniums, and ox-eye daisies, or perhaps an archway or wall covered with a tangle of ramblers and honeysuckle, or a modern plan that mixes ornamental grasses with large shrub roses. This is about letting your garden be a little wild and loose in style.

For a wild garden to work, all the plants in it need to have at least some semblance of wildness. The easiest way to achieve this is to plant wild roses (p.64), and the true species of any perennials and flowering shrubs you want to include. However, these can sometimes be difficult to source, very vigorous, and generally unruly. Wild roses, for example, are generally both tall and broad, often exceeding 6ft (2m) in both directions. For a smaller garden especially, the trick is to find garden hybrids that still look wild and are attractive to wildlife, but which are much less aggressive, smaller, and will repeat-flower. Good roses that answer this description are 'Lupo', 'Ballerina', 'Morning Mist', 'Scented Carpet', 'Center Stage', 'Scabrosa', and 'Fru Dagmar Hastrup'.

Roses with semi-double flowers would also work, as long as they keep the informal, shrubby, often arching growth of the species and aren't too brightly colored. Some of the toughest are once-flowering varieties like *Rosa* x *alba* 'Alba Semiplena', 'Celsiana', *R. gallica* var. *officinalis*, and *R. gallica* 'Versicolor' (*R. mundi*). Some repeat-flowering varieties would also be suitable, especially hybrid musks like 'Penelope', 'Vanity' (although perhaps a little on the bright side), and 'Trier', which all make substantial shrubs, or soft yellow 'Daybreak' and 'Callisto', which are much shorter.

Some of the English roses will fit in perfectly, such as 'Scarborough Fair', 'The Lady's Blush', 'Skylark' (with semi-double, mid-pink flowers), and 'Comte de Champagne'. Other good modern varieties are 'Clair Martin', 'Île de Fleurs', and 'Pink Roadrunner'. All of these look beautiful among other wild or wild-looking plants, but will need a little extra care and attention—they might struggle if grasses and other plants were growing right around their bases.

With enough space, you could allow a rambler to grow freely without any support to make a magnificent heap. The resulting arching growth would encourage even more flowers and, potentially, hips, too. Before planting, clear the area of perennial weeds like thistles, nettles, bindweed, and docks (since extracting them later from a mass of rose stems would be unpleasant). To encourage a little more height, erect a 5–6ft (1.5–2m) triangular or square support for the stems to grow through and arch over. Some suitable varieties would be 'Francis E. Lester', 'Adélaïde d'Orléans', 'Rambling Rector', 'Polyantha Grandiflora', and the less vigorous (and repeat-flowering) 'The Lady of the Lake' and 'Open Arms'.

Meadows with roses

Roses make a great addition to planting plans inspired by natural meadows, used either as boundary hedges (pp.34–35) or to make hummocks or heaps—as they often do naturally in mountain hay meadows. The competition from meadow grasses can benefit species roses by curbing their

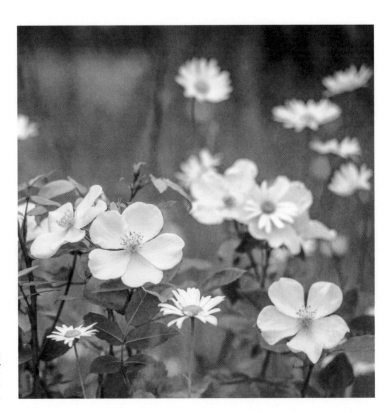

A meadow pairing
The soft yellow blooms of 'Tottering-by-Gently' can be seen here mingling with ox-eye daisies.

Wilder by nature
The large, arching growth of *Rosa* 'Cerise Bouquet' makes a stunning addition to this wildflower meadow in Rockcliffe Garden, Gloucestershire, in the UK.

exuberant growth and giving them a more natural look. They will also be more likely to set a good crop of hips and to develop rich fall colors on their leaves.

It's important to match the potential size of the rose with that of the meadow. If space is limited—say, less than 55ft² (5m²)—short, compact species like *Rosa spinosissima*, *R. nitida*, and *R. gallica* are good choices. If there's a bit more room, try *Rosa rugosa*, *R. palustris*, *R. virginiana*, or *R. woodsii*. Bigger meadows offer the widest choice, including some yellow roses, such as *Rosa xanthina* f. *hugonis*, *R. ecae*, and *R. primula*. Added to these are some excellent near-wild hybrids, including *R. xanthina* 'Canary Bird', 'Cantabrigiensis', and 'Headleyensis'.

There are also many large species roses in white, pink, and red to choose from. Probably the best known and most garden-worthy is 'Geranium', a hybrid of *Rosa moyesii* with bright red flowers and scarlet, flagon-shaped hips. *Rosa setipoda* and *R. sweginzowii* are similar, with generous quantities of paler pink flowers. While the hips of these are very showy, they aren't particularly long-lasting, as they tend to lose their color and plumpness in early winter. Also from China, free-flowering, tough, reliable, and with a good crop of hips are *R. davidii* and *R. multibracteata*. A special mention should be made of a particular form of *R. sericea*—*pteracantha*, which has very large, flattened, bright-red thorns that look dramatic when the sun is shining through them. It needs pruning hard each year, since these thorns only appear on young stems. *R. roxburghii* has showy flowers and hips and makes a fine shrub.

A number of North American and European species make fine large shrubs in a meadow setting. The flowers are all various shades of pink, and their hips are generally longer-lasting than the Chinese species—sometimes lasting right through the winter. *R. californica* and *R. nutkana* come from North America, while *R. villosa*, *R. rubiginosa*, and *R. canina* are native to Europe. There are also a number of excellent species hybrids that retain that wild look and are happy growing in grass: *R.* x *hibernica* from *R. canina*, 'Scarlet Fire' from *R. gallica*, and the Frühlings series, including 'Frühlingsgold', from *R. spinosissima*.

Many garden roses with single or semi-double, wild-looking flowers would also work. *Rosa* x *alba* 'Alba Semiplena', an extraordinarily tough and adaptable rose, is one of the best. 'Violacea' has good-sized, striking, deep-purple blooms, although, sadly, no hips. 'Complicata' is much more modern, first appearing in the early 20th century, but looks perfectly at home in wild areas, the pink flowers being followed by large, rounded hips. Of the repeat-flowering roses, 'Topolina', 'Tottering-By-Gently', and 'The Lady's Blush' would all fit in well and be tough enough to cope with the conditions, although they might need a bit more care and attention—for example, keeping the space immediately around their bases clear and mulched.

Roses for wildlife

With their long flowering season and hips in the fall and winter, roses are some of the best plants to support the type of wildlife that most of us want to attract to our gardens, like bees, hoverflies, small mammals, and birds.

A great variety of insects are fond of visiting the flowers of roses. While they lack nectar, their pollen is highly nutritious: rich in proteins, amino acids, carbohydrates, lipids, and vitamins. Bees—honey, carpenter, and bumble—take this back to their nests to feed their larvae, while other insects—including hoverflies and beetles—eat it while on the flower.

It's easy to assess the potential value to pollinators of a semi-double or double rose by gently parting its petals and looking into the center: if there is a good boss of stamens, there is a good chance the pollen will be collected or eaten. Many insects are willing to wheedle their way in through tight spaces if they think the effort will be worthwhile. The flowers of 'Lady of Shalott', for example, are not too double and their stamens are still easily

A winter feast
The red hips of the dog rose, *Rosa canina*, offer a vital food source for birds over the winter months, when other food sources are scarce.

accessible. In very full blooms, the stamens are transformed into small petals, and so are of no value to insects. Avoid these varieties if your goal is to attract and support wildlife.

Rose hips are hugely valuable to wildlife. They come in a great variety of different shapes, sizes, and colors, and, while some only last a few weeks once ripe, others stay attached through winter, meaning you can offer a supply of hips from midsummer (*R. sericea* and *R. fedtschenkoana*) to the following spring ('Grouse', 'Partridge', and 'Polyantha Grandiflora'). 'Bonica' and 'The Generous Gardener' are unusual in having more double flowers as well as setting a good crop of hips. Siting a rose that keeps its hips through the winter near the house will give you a good view of the birds that come to eat them.

Species roses and ramblers, with their open flowers and abundance of hips, offer the best of both worlds when it comes to supporting wildlife. Ramblers, in particular, can't be beaten in terms of sheer numbers of flowers and hips. On a mature plant of *Rosa filipes* 'Kiftsgate' or 'Francis E. Lester', there will be many, many thousands of flowers followed by a similar number of hips. These are of particular value to birds, since many are just the right size to be picked off one by one and to slip nicely down the gullet, while the mature ramblers' size will provide safety for the birds, since they can perch high above the ground. *Rosa rugosa* and some of its hybrids produce a great crop of lovely, large, juicy, and presumably tasty hips that birds and small mammals relish.

Bee-friendly blooms
The open flowers of the rambler 'Goldfinch' make it easy for bumblebees to access their pollen.

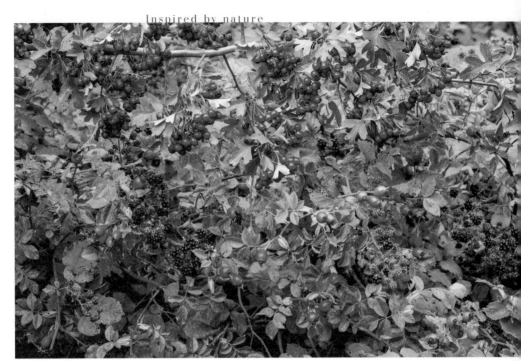

Winter bounty
The scarlet hips of *Rosa rubiginosa,* shown here alongside the darker red hawthorn berries and ripening blackberries, provide a valuable food source for birds through the fall and winter months.

All hips not eaten on the branch will eventually drop off or be removed when the rose is pruned. Leave them on the ground: there, they'll become a good source of food for ground-dwelling creatures, whether mammals or invertebrates, or else will be broken down into organic matter by fungi and soil-dwellers—if they don't develop into seedlings, that is.

A successful wildlife garden will offer plenty of shelter for all kinds of mammals, birds, and insects. In a small space, aim for a tangle of roses on boundary fences—perhaps be freer in how you prune them, so they bush out a little. Or even better, plant a mixed hedge that includes wild-looking roses such as *R. rubiginosa* or *R. glauca* mixed with other shrubs and climbers attractive to wildlife, such as honeysuckle, blackthorn, hawthorn, and field maple. If you have space, a thicket or hummock of roses (p.53) will also be a valuable habitat.

In addition to insects that collect and eat their pollen and assorted creatures that eat their hips, roses are beloved by a huge array of seemingly less attractive visitors: aphids that suck their sap; bees, beetles, and caterpillars that eat their leaves; and occasionally insects that bore into their stems. While all these harm roses, they're also food for other creatures. Aphids are a classic example that can multiply at a frightening pace, but a healthy population of beneficial insects and birds will happily keep them in check. The aphids are an important part of the garden ecosystem, which is why it is so important that, unless absolutely necessary, they are not controlled artificially using insecticides or any other means.

"Look out for signs of the leaf-cutter bee: its beautifully excised leaf cuts should be admired."

ROSE

types

The evolution of garden roses

Most of the development of the huge range of flower-forms, colors, growth habits, and scents in the roses available today has happened in the last 200 years.

Plants started appearing about 500 million years ago, but fossils found in Asia suggest that it wasn't until the Eocene period, about 35 million years ago, that roses first evolved. Other fossils found in Colorado and Oregon have been identified as being possibly *Rosa nutkana* and *R. palustris*, both still common in North America. Today, there are estimated to be about 150 species of wild roses, but only eight of them have been widely used in the development of the many thousands of garden roses that have been introduced.

Initially, any new roses would have been the result of chance crosses that appeared in gardens, or mutations of existing roses. During the 18th and early 19th centuries, rose breeders developed large-scale breeding programs, comparable to the breeders of today, who grow over 100,000 seedlings each year. All of their plants, however, would have been the chance crosses produced by the natural inclination of bees as they visited flowers in succession. It wasn't until the middle of the 19th century that specific varieties were crossed with the idea of a certain goal in mind. English nurseryman William Paul was one of the early rose breeders, although one gets the impression that he regarded the whole process as a bit too tricky and long-winded, since after a time he gave up noting parents.

This new, more scientific approach really took off with François Lacharme of Lyon (whose only well-known rose today is 'Madame Plantier', p.175) and Englishman Henry Bennett (whose best-known rose is 'Mrs. John Laing'). The latter was a cattle farmer from Wiltshire who was familiar with strict breeding programs designed to produce better offspring. He set

Living history
These three varieties show the characteristics of roses through the ages, from a near-species hybrid (left), through an early modern hybrid (center), to a modern hybrid (right).

Rosa gallica var. officinalis

'Président de Sèze'

'Royal William'

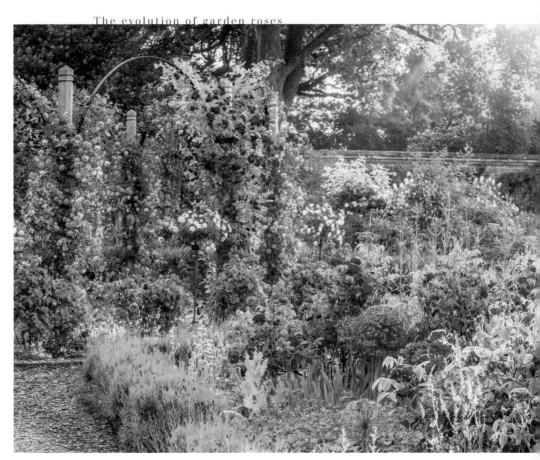

Diversity of form
Standard, rambler, and shrub roses in the gardens of Mottisfont Abbey, UK.

up state-of-the-art facilities with heated greenhouses, and in 1879 introduced ten "Pedigree Hybrids of the Tea Rose," which in 1890 were renamed "hybrid teas." (Although the parents aren't known for sure, the first generally recognized hybrid tea, 'La France', was bred by Jean-Baptiste Guillot (Fils) and introduced in 1867.)

Since then, the breeding of roses has become very sophisticated, although the same basic process is used in most cases: a knife or scissors to harvest the stamens and a paint brush to apply the pollen. A computer has become invaluable for determining the best parents and crosses. Each year, the biggest breeders make more than 100,000 crosses, using more than 100 different parents to produce several hundred thousand seeds. The resulting seedlings are then trialed for several years before the final decision is made as to which to introduce. The whole process usually takes ten years from crossing to introduction. Careful record-taking at each stage is crucial to producing better varieties. The chances of creating something better and significantly different than either of the parents is extremely small, and when a promising new rose is identified, it has to be increased in number from the initial one to the many plants needed to introduce it to the world.

Species roses & their hybrids

Wild roses have the simplest flowers. They are full of character and thrive in a wide range of situations, although most need space to do their best.

Roses are only native to regions north of the equator, from North America across Europe, North Africa, and the Middle East to Asia. There are about 150 species, mostly in Asia (the variations within each species and their readiness to hybridize with each other makes counting them difficult). The dog rose, *Rosa canina*, for example, can reproduce asexually and so botanists disagree as to whether to treat it as one species or a huge number of different ones.

The great majority of wild roses are various shades of pink or white, with a few reds and yellows. With the exception of the *Rosa sericea* group, each of which has four, all of them have five petals. Fragrance is variable in strength and type, as is habit and height, with *Rosa spinosissima* being one of the shortest, only about 6in (15cm) tall when growing on sand dunes and exposed to strong winds. By contrast, some of the big climbing species native to warm parts of Asia can reach 50ft (15m) to the top of large trees.

Most species roses only flower once in a season. The exceptions include *R. rugosa*, *R. bracteata*, and *R. fedtschenkoana*. Wild rose hips are variable in size, shape, and color. Some stay attached for many months, while others drop off almost as soon as they are ripe.

A number of wild roses are very garden-worthy—for example, *R. moyesii*, *R. roxburghii*, and *R. glauca*—and look superb growing in long grass or up into trees. They need little or no maintenance and shouldn't be pruned at all. All, of course, are excellent for wildlife, providing pollen, fruit, and safe shelter in their thorny thickets.

Rosa glauca

Rosa bracteata

R. x cantabrigiensis (yellow blooms, left) accompanied by topiary balls and surrounded by cow parsley and forget-me-nots

Rugosas

One of the most useful species roses, *Rosa rugosa* is native to the coasts of northern Japan, North Korea, northeastern China, and Siberia, and so is incredibly winter-hardy and tolerant of salt-laden winds. It is also free of disease and able to cope with poor soils. Its fragrance is strong and exactly like that of the old roses. It also has the ability—rare in wild roses—of being able to repeat-flower, the flowers being followed by large hips. It is not surprising that it has been used extensively in breeding programs.

The best of its hybrids are as healthy and winter-hardy as their parent, grow well in hot or cooler summers, and have flowers varying from single to fully double. The great majority are various shades of pink, white, and purple, with some of the best being 'Hansa' (p.147), 'Roseraie de l'Haÿ' and 'Blanche Double de Coubert'. There are a few in shades of apricot and yellow, such as 'Agnes'. Some still bear the large hips of the species. Unfortunately, some varieties are not as resistant to disease, especially rust, as *Rosa rugosa*. Most are large shrubs, 6ft (2m) or more, but recently some short shrubs, less than 3ft (1m) tall, have been introduced.

'Roseraie de l'Haÿ'

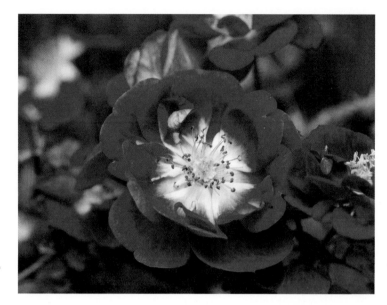

Rosa spinosissima 'William III'

Spinosissimas

Rosa spinosissima is an extremely tough rose native from Iceland across Europe and Asia, and even into North Africa. It has many synonyms, most commonly *R. pimpinellifolia*, and is also known as the Scotch or burnet rose. It is often seen growing by the sea, where it grows no more than 6in (15cm) tall, although in better conditions it reaches 3ft (1m). It is thorny, with small leaves. The small white flowers are produced early, have a lovely lily-of-the-valley fragrance, and are followed by round black hips and often a superb display of fall color on the leaves.

During the first half of the 19th century, hundreds of forms and hybrids were selected and introduced. While nearly all have small flowers, they vary in number of petals from five (the very beautiful 'Dunwich Rose') to a few dozen (the double, white-flowered form), and in color from white through all shades of pink ('Andrewsii') to purple ('William III') as well as yellow (*R.* x *harrisonii* 'Williams' Double Yellow'). Some are bicolored with a different color on the reverse ('Single Cherry') or two shades on each petal ('Marbled Pink').

None of these older varieties repeat-flower except 'Stanwell Perpetual', a lovely rose with large, very double, strongly scented blooms. More recently, new interest in the spinosissimas has resulted in some repeat-flowering varieties being introduced, such as 'Silas Marner' (p.157) and 'Peter Boyd', named after the world authority on them.

"An incredibly tough rose, *R. spinosissima* can be found growing on sand dunes in the wild."

The oldest garden roses

These roses have one flush of many-petaled flowers each year. Most have an "old rose" fragrance—the rich scent that's most associated with roses.

Gallicas

The gallicas are the oldest of the garden roses. They originated from *Rosa gallica*, a short, suckering rose native to southern and central Europe, with pale pink to red flowers and often a strong, delicious fragrance. Its hybrids are characterized by dark foliage, the almost complete absence of thorns, and flowers mostly in shades of mid-pink to purple, with a number having striped petals. Many have a wonderfully rich fragrance.

The oldest of the gallicas and so, most probably, of cultivated roses is *R. gallica* var. *officinalis*, which may date back to Roman times. It became hugely important in France from the Middle Ages, being grown in great quantities for its medicinal, culinary, and cosmetic properties. *Rosa gallica* 'Versicolor' (also known as *R. mundi*) is a striped sport (spontaneous genetic mutation) dating from the 16th century.

Most gallicas were bred in the 19th century in France, some of the better ones being 'Tuscany Superb', 'Charles de Mills' (p.195), 'Président de Sèze', and 'Ipsilanté' (p.113). They are generally tough, reliable, and easy to grow. They are effective in mixed borders, but some can sucker freely.

'Charles de Mills'

'Celsiana'

Damasks

The damasks, like the gallicas and albas, are an ancient group, all once-flowering with one intriguing exception. They are usually easy to distinguish from the gallicas with their laxer growth, pricklier stems, paler green leaves, and white or paler pink flowers. They are typically more strongly and deliciously fragrant than the gallicas, too: it is from a group of damasks (collectively called 'Kazanlik') that the essential oil attar of roses is distilled.

Their origin is a bit of a mystery. DNA analysis suggests that they are a product of three parents: *Rosa gallica*, *R. moschata*, and *R. fedtschenkoana*. Pollen from *R. gallica* fertilized the ovule of *R. moschata* to produce a hybrid rose, which in turn acted as a seed parent, using pollen from *R. fedtschenkoana*. While roses generally happily cross with each other, how did these three get together in the first place? They do not naturally grow in the same areas. Perhaps it all happened in someone's garden.

'Quatre Saisons' is the only old rose to repeat-flower; it is possibly the same long-flowering rose we are told was growing in ancient Greek and Roman times (pp.8–11). There are also wonderful once-flowering damasks, including 'Madame Hardy' (p.110), 'Ispahan' (p.146), and 'Celsiana'.

"Of an estimated 150 wild rose species, only eight have been widely used to develop the garden roses we see today."

Rosa x alba 'Alba Semiplena'

'Fantin-Latour'

Albas

Albas are perhaps the most distinct of the three most ancient types of roses, with gray-green leaves, sturdy, upright growth, and white or pale pink flowers. Many of them have superb fragrance. *Rosa x alba* 'Alba Semiplena' is probably also one of the earliest roses to have been cultivated in gardens, possibly as far back as Roman times—no doubt for its excellent crop of hips as well as its beautiful blooms and exquisite scent.

DNA analysis indicates that albas are crosses between varieties of *Rosa gallica* and *R. canina*. They are a tough group, able to survive poor conditions and years of neglect. They are some of the best roses for shady positions and look lovely mixed in with other plants. Most varieties were bred in the 19th century, with some of the best being 'Alba Maxima', 'Königin von Dänemark' (p.149), and 'Great Maiden's Blush' (p.115).

Centifolias

The centifolias are perhaps the least garden-worthy of the once-flowering old roses. Their growth is often difficult to manage, their flowers are a little too heavy, and their health is not great. But, of course, there are exceptions, and both *Rosa x centifolia* (the original variety) and 'Fantin-Latour' have beautiful flowers. Fragrance is variable, but very good in some.

Centifolias date back to the late 16th century, and are probably the result of a cross made in Holland between various gallicas and damasks. The original centifolia often features in Dutch and Flemish flower paintings. It is rather unkindly known as the cabbage rose, although old herbalists called it the queen of roses. A number of centifolias are unusual sports—some dwarfs (*R. x centifolia* 'De Meaux'), one with a flower bud like Napoleon's hat (*R. x c.* 'Cristata', or 'Chapeau de Napoléon'), and—most famously—moss roses.

Mosses

These roses are characterized by mossy growth around their flower buds and in some cases down their stems. It feels sticky when rubbed and has a delicious, resinous smell. This moss was found originally on sports in the damask and centifolia groups of roses; the former producing brown moss, the latter green moss. It was first spotted in the middle of the 17th century in France, probably on the rose we now call *Rosa* x *centifolia* 'Muscosa' or 'Old Pink Moss'. It wasn't until the middle of the 19th century that breeders, particularly Philippe-Victor Verdier in France, developed new varieties. The Victorians loved them.

As might be expected from their parentage—both damasks and centifolias—the mosses are a mixed group of roses. They are nearly all once-flowering, but a few, resulting from crosses with Chinas (p.72), repeat-flower well ('Mousseline' is the best). Unfortunately, mosses aren't especially disease-resistant. Most are shades of pink, with a few being white, purple, or striped. The darkest is the upright and short 'Nuits de Young'. 'William Lobb' (p.161) is paler and extremely vigorous, and it can be grown as a climber. Its crimson-purple flowers fade to lavender and eventually almost gray.

William Lobb

Repeat-flowering old roses

These roses all have their origins in China, and some flower throughout the season. The colors include apricot and yellow, and there is a wide variety of fragrances.

Chinas

The Chinese had been growing and breeding roses for a very long time before any of their varieties were exported to the West. 'Old Blush China' (also known as 'Parson's Pink', and now as *Rosa* x *odorata* 'Pallida'), for example, had been grown in China and possibly Japan for at least a thousand years, valued for its continuous flowering. It was one of the first two Chinas to come to Europe, probably in the middle of the 18th century, the other being 'Slater's Crimson' (now *R. chinensis* 'Semperflorens'). These were followed by *R.* x *odorata* 'Hume's Blush Tea-scented China' in 1809, and finally 'Parks' Yellow China' in 1824.

More Chinas were developed from these initial introductions, mostly in France. As a group, they are characterized by light, airy growth and single, semi-double, or loosely double flowers, mostly in shades of white, pink, and red; although, for the first time in hybrid roses, we see some soft yellow and apricot colors in *R.* x *odorata* 'Mutabilis' (p.178) and 'Comtesse du Cayla'.

Given a warm position, some of the Chinas will flower all year round, as does *R.* x *odorata* 'Bengal Crimson' in the Chelsea Physic Garden in London.

R. x *odorata* 'Mutabilis'

'Louise Odier'

Bourbons

A few years after Chinese roses first reached Europe, on the Île de Bourbon (now known as Réunion) in the Indian Ocean, colonial farmers grew 'Old Blush China' and 'Quatre Saisons' side by side in hedges. A different-looking seedling appeared close by and was spotted by a Monsieur Perichon. Seeds from it were sent back to France, and the resulting rose was much admired for its rich pink blooms and ability to repeat-flower. It was introduced in 1823 under the name of 'Le Rosier de l'Île de Bourbon'.

This rose was passed around, new varieties were swiftly bred from it, and so the Bourbon roses were born. Nearly all are pink, a few red or white, and several striped. Most have strongly fragrant, many-petaled flowers very much in the style of the old roses, but you can see the beginnings of modern roses in their leaves and stems, which look like those of the hybrid teas. Almost all of them repeat-flower. Unfortunately, they are quite susceptible to blackspot, powdery mildew, and rust. The flowers of most varieties also spoil badly in the rain. 'Louise Odier' and 'Madame Isaac Péreire' are perhaps the two best.

'Portlandica'

'Ferdinand Pichard'

Portlands

The Portlands are a relatively small but select group, well worth a place in the garden for their beauty, fragrance, repeat-flowering, and general health. The original Portland rose (also known as 'Portlandica', 'Paestana', or 'Portland Crimson Monthly Rose') dates back at least to 1783. It repeat-flowers, has dark pink or pale crimson semi-double flowers, and was probably a cross between *Rosa gallica* var. *officinalis* and 'Quatre Saisons'.

Portlands are much more upright and sturdy in habit than damasks, with short flower stems. They are perfect for mixing in with other plants, in formal settings, or even as a hedge. Most are pink, but there are some very dark ones like 'Indigo', while 'Marbrée' has deep purple flowers mottled with paler pink. There are three particularly garden-worthy ones: 'Jacques Cartier' (p.144), 'Comte de Chambord' (p.97), and 'Rose de Rescht'.

Hybrid perpetuals

The hybrid perpetuals are the result of crossing various roses from a wide variety of groups including Portlands, hybrid Chinas, and Bourbons. Many were introduced in the late 19th century, when flower shows were popular and the ideal in a rose to exhibit was the perfection of its bud. Most breeders were intent on perfecting the beauty and shape of the flowers with little regard for the overall shape of the plant or its health—they thought nothing of using extremely toxic pesticides to keep their roses free of pests and diseases. As a result, many of the varieties are rather coarse shrubs or climbers with poor disease resistance.

The flowers are all shades of white, pink, and red. 'Ferdinand Pichard' is striped pink and red, and 'Roger Lambelin' red splashed with white. The strongly fragrant 'Souvenir du Docteur Jamain' is a wonderfully rich dark crimson but doesn't flower freely and makes a sparse, lanky climber. 'Paul Neyron' boasts some of the largest flowers to be found in the rose world. 'Reine des Violettes', 'Duke of Edinburgh', and 'Ferdinand Pichard' are perhaps the three best.

Tea roses

The tea roses are the result of crossing *Rosa* × *odorata* 'Hume's Blush Tea-scented China' and 'Parks' Yellow China' with various Bourbons and noisettes, the first—'Adam'—being introduced in 1835. The flowers have a delicate charm in which one can see the beginnings of the hybrid-tea bloom, with its high, pointed center. Those that are very double (like 'Maman Cochet' (p.187) and 'Devoniensis') open up to look much like the old roses, with beautifully arranged petals. They were originally called "tea-scented China roses," since they smelled like a freshly opened packet of China tea. This scent may be mixed with a wide range of others, including violet, freesia, carnation, citrus, banana, and camphor.

Tea roses vary greatly in color and include for the first time in hybrid roses a true, rich yellow ('Perle des Jardins') and apricot ('Lady Hillingdon'). They vary greatly in size, too, from small bushes to tall climbers, although their eventual height is much affected by climate and soil. They love the heat and flower nearly all year round in warm places. In cooler climates, they are much less satisfactory and struggle to grow and flower.

Polyanthas

The polyanthas are not a well-known group, but they do include some pretty, garden-worthy varieties. Typically, they have small, double, white or pink flowers on a short, quite compact shrub. Their common parent is *Rosa multiflora* (formerly known as *R. polyantha*)—a vigorous rambler with small white fragrant flowers that is happy to cross with most other roses, seeding itself around with gay abandon. The first recognized polyantha, 'Pâquerette', was introduced in 1875 by Jean-Baptiste Guillot (Fils) and probably has 'Old Blush China' in its background.

Those in vivid colors include the 'Orléans Rose', with open, cherry-red, white-centered flowers. This produced many sports, including crimson 'Miss Edith Cavell', and has also been important in the breeding of nearly all polyanthas and floribundas. Other brightly colored polyanthas include orange-scarlet 'Paul Crampel' and purple 'Baby Faurax'.

Most polyanthas have no fragrance, but there are exceptions, such as 'Marie Pavié' (p.123). The best known polyantha is 'Cécile Brunner' (p.216), whose pink flower buds are like those on a perfect miniature hybrid tea. All polyanthas repeat-flower well and will associate beautifully with other plants in mixed borders.

'Climbing Lady Hillingdon'

'Cécile Brunner'

Modern roses

From the middle of the 19th century, scientific breeding methods produced a wider range of colors and forms in roses, and repeat-flowering became common.

Hybrid teas

Originally these were the result of crosses between a tea rose (for the flower form) and a hybrid perpetual (for vigor) in the 1860s. The early varieties were beautiful at both the bud and open-flower stages, and their growth was quite bushy; but breeders focused purely on making the buds more classically beautiful, with a high, pointed center. The fully open flowers of the new varieties often lacked definition and were not particularly attractive.

Hybrid teas were a plant of their time, with their bright colors, suitability for mass planting, and—as pesticides were widely used with impunity—less than perfect health. As tastes changed and gardeners demanded roses with good disease resistance, they fell out of favor. The most famous hybrid tea is 'Peace', introduced in 1945, and partly responsible for the huge boost in the popularity of roses in the 1940s and 50s. It is in the background of great numbers of subsequent varieties. 'Warm Wishes', with its high-pointed center and perfectly arranged outer petals, is another classic example.

'Warm Wishes'

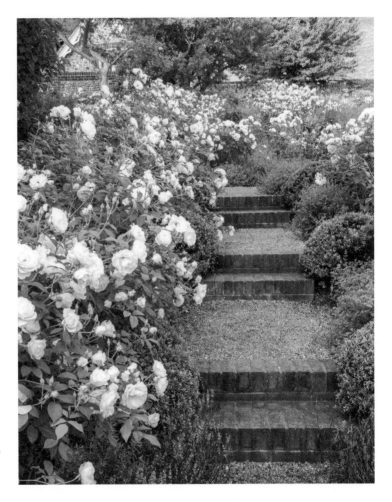

'Iceberg'

Floribundas

The breeders who developed the floribundas were looking for a mass of color on a tough, winter-hardy bush. The form of the flower and the fragrance were less important. The first varieties were bred by D. T. Poulsen in Denmark, who crossed polyanthas with hybrid teas. He introduced 'Red Riding Hood' (or 'Rödhätte') in 1912, but it wasn't until after World War I that other breeders around the world joined in and floribundas (known at first as hybrid polyanthas) became popular. As tastes changed, the individual flowers became more hybrid tealike.

'Iceberg' (p.185) is easily the most famous of the floribundas (even though, strictly speaking, it's a hybrid musk). 'Trumpeter' is a classic 1970s floribunda, with loosely double flowers of an almost fluorescent orange-red.

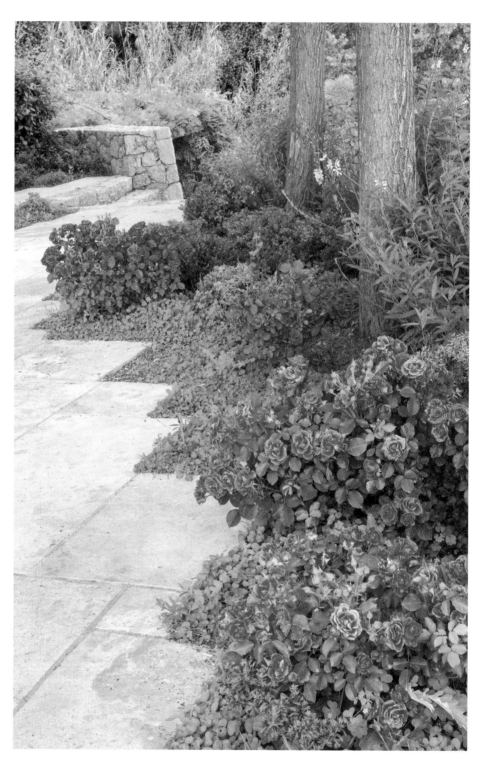

Low-growing beauty Vivid pink patio roses soften the edge of this paved limestone path.

"While a small rose
variety can get lost in a
mixed bed, if planted into
a container, it becomes a
true focal point."

Patio roses

Patio roses—also known as minifloras and dwarf cluster-flowered—are somewhere between floribundas and miniature roses: about 2ft (60cm) tall, with flowers about 2in (5cm) across. Both plant and flower size are intermediate. They flower freely and are useful for the edge of a border or for containers. They come from a very mixed background, and so the flowers vary greatly in number of petals and color. 'Queen Mother' is one of the best known, with soft-pink, semi-double flowers. 'Sweet Dream' has very full peach-colored flowers, and 'Marlena' is semi-double and scarlet.

Miniature roses

These are the smallest roses, usually less than 2ft (60cm) tall, with flowers that are only about 1in (2.5cm) across. While they can be grown in the ground, they are ideal for containers, where it is easier to appreciate their often pretty flowers, some of them perfect old rose-style rosettes. The original miniature roses probably came from China around 1800. A number of varieties were bred, but they didn't become popular until in 1918, when a perpetual-flowering dwarf rose was found in Switzerland and named 'Rouletii'. Soon, many new varieties bred from it—including 'Para Ti' (also known as 'Pour Toi') by Pedro Dot in Spain.

The remarkable California rose breeder Ralph Moore introduced many miniatures, including 'Stars 'n' Stripes' and 'Little Flirt', in the second half of the 20th century. In Europe, they are mostly seen as potted plants, bought as a colorful, but perhaps short-lived, present. Poulsen Roses of Denmark developed varieties that can be grown easily from cuttings, flower 12 months of the year, and withstand the rigors of being transported long distances in trucks.

'Pour Toi'

Hybrid musks

Most hybrid musks have small- to medium-sized flowers in large sprays in shades of white, pink, yellow, or buff, with a fruity, musky fragrance. The best-known ones—'Penelope' (p.107), 'Cornelia', 'Felicia' (p.111), and 'Buff Beauty'—make large shrubs at least 6ft (2m) tall and across, and which in warm climates can make substantial climbers.

In the early 20th century, the Reverend Joseph Pemberton, an avid exhibitor of the rather fussy hybrid perpetuals (p.74), decided to try and breed roses that would be tougher and easier to grow. He started with 'Trier', a large shrub with fragrant, small, nearly single white flowers, as well as various polyanthas, hybrid teas, teas, and noisettes. The first three varieties above were bred by him. More recently, Louis Lens in Belgium used dwarf *Rosa multiflora* and *R. helenae* hybrids to produce short, repeat-flowering, hardy shrubs and ramblers such as 'Guirlande d'Amour' (p.213) and 'Sibelius'. His successors, Rudy and Ann Velle, have produced some lovely, scented, healthy varieties, including 'Caroline's Heart' and 'Fil des Saisons'.

Must-have hybrid musk
The soft apricot buds and white blooms of 'Penelope' (right) are paired with the brighter apricot 'Just Joey' beneath two pleached lime trees.

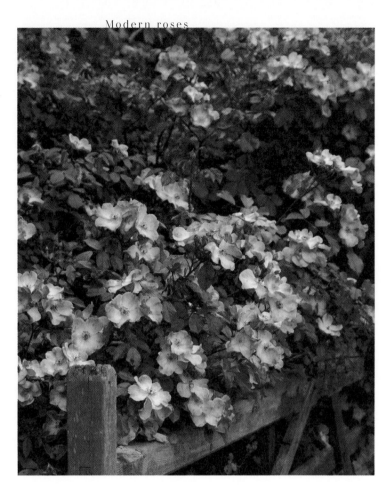

'Rosy Cushion'

Modern shrub roses

This group encompasses a wide range of varieties bred in the 20th and 21st centuries, originally arising from crosses of various species roses with hybrid teas and floribundas. There is no common denominator to them: flower size ranges from small to very large, number of petals from five to more than 100, and fragrance from none to strong. Some are short, others tall; some repeat-flower, while others don't. In general, though, they are tough roses that grow well in less than ideal conditions.

More recently, modern shrub roses have improved greatly, and many make good garden plants. 'Frühlingsgold', 'Nevada', and 'Rosy Cushion' are good older varieties. The German breeders Kordes have been responsible for many excellent recent varieties, such as 'Lemon Fizz' (p.126), 'Summer Memories' (p.114), and 'Île de Fleurs'. Mention must also be made of the Knock Out series bred by Bill Radler in the United States. The original 'Knock Out' was introduced in 2000, and many millions have been sold in North America. It has been followed by a number of others, including 'Pink Knock Out', 'Double Knock Out' (p.166), and 'Sunny Knock Out'.

English roses

The English roses were developed by British breeder David Austin, his ambition being to create varieties that had the charm and fragrance of old roses combined with the repeat-flowering and wide color range of modern roses. He started by crossing old roses with various hybrid teas and floribundas, which led to a small group of once-flowering roses including his first well-known variety, 'Constance Spry' (p.146), in 1961.

Austin's roses slowly became better known and received a big boost in 1983 when he introduced three varieties at the Chelsea Flower Show: 'Mary Rose', 'Heritage', and the one most responsible for English roses becoming well-known, not only in the UK, but also in North America, Europe, and Australasia, 'Graham Thomas' (p.144).

Gertrude Jekyll, with its very strong, old -ose fragrance, was introduced in 1986, while newer varieties include 'Roald Dahl' (p.90, p.153), 'Gabriel Oak' (p.100), 'Eustacia Vye' (p.109), and 'Desdemona' (p.109, p.123). These have become extremely popular around the world due to their overall beauty, fragrance, and, increasingly, their health. There are a number of climbers and repeat-flowering ramblers among the English roses.

Ground-cover roses

These ground-hugging roses are usually no more than 18in (50cm) tall and very variable in how far they spread. They form a thick mat that supposedly prevents weeds from growing through them. Weeds, though, are not easily deterred, and they will soon grow through, giving you the unpleasant job of extracting them from between thorny stems.

Ground-cover roses are perhaps better seen as free-flowering, short-growing, mound-forming roses, suitable for the edge of a border or path, or for growing in a container where they will trail attractively over the rim. All have small flowers, usually produced continuously over a long season. Some, such as 'Grouse', 'Partridge', and 'Alexander von Humboldt', will produce an excellent crop of hips. Most have little or no scent, but some good exceptions are 'Center Stage', 'Scented Carpet', 'Grouse', and 'Partridge'. When the first of the Flower Carpet series was introduced in 1989, it attracted much attention for its bright pink flowers and excellent health, as well as for the bright pink pot it was sold in. Its breeder, Noack of Germany, has since introduced a number of others in different colors, with 'Flower Carpet White' being perhaps the best.

'Flower Carpet White'

Climbing roses

This is a very variable group of roses, coming from a great mix of parentages, all having the propensity to climb, but varying in height, stiffness, and ability to repeat-flower.

'Blush Noisette'

'Climbing Madame Caroline Testout'

Noisettes

These are some of the most beautiful climbers for a warmer, Mediterranean-type climate. The first of them, a cross between the vigorous climbing species *Rosa moschata* and 'Old Blush China', was called 'Champney's Pink Cluster'. This was probably a chance seedling that grew in John Champney's garden in South Carolina in the early 1800s. A local nurseryman, Philippe Noisette, collected seed from it and grew a shorter, continuously flowering rose that he named 'Blush Noisette'. The flowers of most varieties bred from this are loosely or fully double, medium to large, come in a wide range of colors, and often have a lovely fragrance. A number of them, like 'Rêve d'Or' and 'Crépuscule' (p.180), are yellow or apricot, achieved by crossing 'Blush Noisette' with 'Parks' Yellow China'.

'Madame Alfred Carrière' (p.188) is probably both the best known and hardiest of the noisettes: it has highly fragrant, large, cupped, blush-pink flowers and is very vigorous, needing plenty of space.

Climbers

While a climbing rose is easy to define—a rose that grows to a height of between 6ft (2m) and 33ft (10m)—the propensity of a variety to climb will depend very much on the climate and how it is pruned. A shrub in a cooler climate can easily become a climber in a warmer one. Likewise, a lightly pruned shrub growing against a wall, even in a cooler climate, can easily be encouraged to climb up.

Most climbers have large flowers and stiff growth, are not too vigorous, and repeat-flower—although there are a number of exceptions. Climbing roses come, often as sports, from many different groups, including noisettes, hybrid teas, floribundas, ramblers, English roses, Bourbons, teas, Chinas, and hybrid perpetuals. So they are hugely variable, encompassing every size of flower, number of petals, type of fragrance, number of thorns, winter hardiness, and vigor. They are an immensely valuable group of plants, able to grow up and adorn a wide range of structures (pp.170–75, pp.188–93, 198–219) for recommended varieties for various situations).

Ramblers

Ramblers generally have small flowers, lax growth, and do not repeat-flower. With their often extreme vigor, their main value is for growing up trees or over pergolas, where their flowers will hang down in festoons. The less vigorous varieties can also be grown against walls.

The early ramblers were simply crosses between climbing species like *Rosa wichurana*, *R. sempervirens*, *R. moschata*, *R. arvensis*, and *R. multiflora*, and various teas, hybrid perpetuals, and hybrid teas. This resulted in a wide range of different colors, flower sizes, and scents. *R. sempervirens* is more or less evergreen, and this has been passed on to some of its offspring, especially 'Félicité Perpétue' and the very beautiful 'Adélaïde d'Orléans'.

Modern breeding has succeeded in introducing repeat-flowering in a number of varieties (including 'The Lady of the Lake' and 'Gardens of Hex'). This usually means less vigor, and so a rambler that is easier to manage and place in the garden.

A number of ramblers, especially the bigger ones closest to the species like 'Francis E. Lester' (p.215), 'Rambling Rector', (p.150, p.216), and *R. filipes* 'Kiftsgate' (p.215), set a superb crop of orange or red hips, some of which will last well into the winter.

ROSE selector

Choosing the ideal rose

Since roses can play a dominant role in a garden, often living 15 to 20 years or more, it is worth searching for varieties that are best-suited for their intended positions and conditions.

Look for roses with character, that will create the atmosphere you want—a wild thicket of single flowers followed by bright hips, perhaps; the romance and fragrance of old roses; or the exquisite formality of hybrid teas. What colors will work best? Pastel harmonies, or vivid contrasts?

Is repeat-flowering essential? Many roses can be in flower from early summer to late fall. But once-flowering varieties are often full of charm and may be covered in hips through the fall and winter—if they're not eaten by birds.

Where you want to plant the rose is also crucial: if the soil isn't as good as it might be, or if it gets only a few hours of full sun each day, or is against a sun-baked wall, you'll need to select tough, disease-resistant varieties best-suited to those situations. It's also important to choose a rose of the right size—big enough to fill its spot, but not so big you're forever having to cut it back.

If you have the opportunity, seeing roses growing in a garden is always the best way to assess them. You want the whole plant to look good—individual flowers may look stunning in photographs, but if they grow on an awkward-looking bush, they may need some camouflage. Perhaps you'll find the color isn't quite the shade you're after, or that the fragrance is so seductive that you'll want to rethink your entire planting scheme to showcase it.

Sourcing roses

I have included a wide range of roses in this chapter. Some are commonly available in garden centers, others only from specialty nurseries. I wanted to include those I think are the very best for each category, and so a few roses appear multiple times: 'Gertrude Jekyll', for example, has a fabulous old-rose perfume (p.146), but it also makes an excellent short climber to grow up a wall (p.213).

Many entries include the original cultivar name (appellation) that a rose was first registered under, which may help when tracking it down.

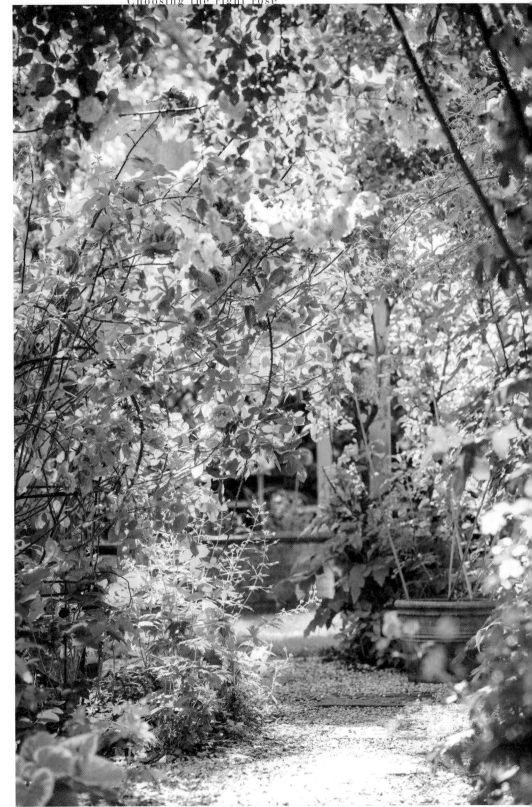

A rose-lover's garden
An assortment of varieties, including 'Nahema' and 'Gertrude Jekyll', cover a pergola in this private London garden.

Roses for the front of a border

This is a great spot for smaller roses, especially ones with good fragrance. It's easy to fully appreciate a rose's beauty when it is planted at the front of the border. Shorter varieties won't get lost here, although some height variation will add interest.

Poseidon

HEIGHT *3½ft (110cm)*   SPREAD *2½ft (75cm)*
FLOWERING *Repeat*   TYPE *Floribunda*   SCENT *Light fruity*
CULTIVAR *'Korfriedhar'*   ZONES *5–10*

An impressive rose with big flowers and an unusual color. Most floribundas have medium-sized, fairly loose flowers, but these are big, up to 3–4in (8–10cm) across. Full-petaled, with rich lavender coloring, they make a big impression in a border. An award-winner for its health. Excellent for both formal and mixed borders.

Roald Dahl

HEIGHT *3ft (1m)*   SPREAD *3ft (1m)*   FLOWERING *Repeat*
TYPE *David Austin English rose*   SCENT *Medium tea*
CULTIVAR *'Ausowlish'*   ZONES *5–11*

A lovely rounded shrub perfect for mixed borders, in a formal planting scheme, or as a hedge. The buds start a rich orange-red, then open into rounded soft-apricot flowers that are produced freely over a long period. With few thorns and excellent health, this rose is a delight.

'Poseidon'

'Roald Dahl'

'Anne Boleyn'

'Scarborough Fair'

Scarborough Fair

HEIGHT *3ft (1m)* SPREAD *3ft (1m)* FLOWERING *Repeat*
TYPE *David Austin English rose* SCENT *Medium musky
old rose* CULTIVAR *'Ausoran'* ZONES *5–11*

An unassuming but pretty rose that produces flowers
from the ground up on a rounded shrub. The blush-pink
flowers have only about 15 petals and are very open,
showing off a central boss of bright yellow stamens. A
particularly good choice at the front of a mixed border,
where its soft coloring will go well with any other
flowers—even yellows. The fragrance is of medium
strength, with old rose coming from the petals and
musk from the stamens.

Anne Boleyn

HEIGHT *3ft (100cm)* SPREAD *3ft (100cm)* FLOWERING
Repeat TYPE *David Austin English rose* SCENT *Light to
medium* CULTIVAR *'Ausecret'* ZONES *5–11*

'Anne Boleyn' has the full-petaled flowers of the classic
English rose; although, with the growth habit being more
arching, it stays fairly short, and so is perfect for the front of
the border. With its soft pink-apricot coloring, it is easy to
incorporate into a wide range of other plants of just about
any color.

Molineux

HEIGHT *3ft (100cm)* SPREAD *2½ft (75cm)* FLOWERING *Repeat*
TYPE *David Austin English rose* SCENT *Light to medium tea*
CULTIVAR *'Ausmol'* ZONES *6–11*

A neat and upright rose particularly good for more formal
plantings. The flowers, which form tight, many-petaled
rosettes, are produced freely and have a tea fragrance with a
musky background. While 'Molineux' is good planted en
masse, it also mixes well with other plants that soften its
upright shape, such as *Nepeta* (catmint); their colors also
complement each other beautifully.

Sweet Fragrance

HEIGHT *3ft (100cm)* SPREAD *2ft (60cm)* FLOWERING *Repeat*
TYPE *Modern shrub* SCENT *Strong sweet* CULTIVAR *'Baince'*
ZONES *5–9*

A lovely rose with many excellent qualities. The medium-to-
large flowers start with the high-pointed center of the classic
hybrid tea, gradually opening to reveal the stamens. They
start as a rich coral-orange, with yellow bases toward the
petals, then pale to a softer salmon pink. With its upright
stems, it makes a very good cut flower. It is particularly
winter-hardy and disease-resistant.

'Molineux'

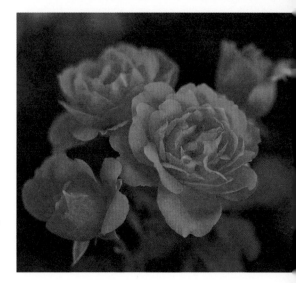

'Sweet Fragrance'

Chi

HEIGHT *3ft (1m)*   SPREAD *3½ft (1.1m)*
FLOWERING *Repeat*   TYPE *Shrub*   SCENT *None*
CULTIVAR *'Baillim'*   ZONES *5–7*

This Easy Elegance rose (see right) was bred by Ping Lim, who has made great strides in breeding healthy, winter-hardy varieties. The true-red flowers are small and fully double, resembling an historic rose, with the petals beautifully arranged in a rosette. It flowers freely and makes a compact shrub slightly wider than it is tall.

Rise 'n' Shine

HEIGHT *2ft (60cm)*   SPREAD *1ft (30cm)*
FLOWERING *Repeat*   TYPE *Miniature*
SCENT *Strong tea*   ZONES *5–11*

'Rise 'n Shine' was bred by Ralph Moore and introduced in 1977. He was a great innovator, making a huge variety of crosses and, in the process, introducing interesting and worthwhile varieties. He was well-known for his miniatures, and this is an excellent example, especially as it is fragrant, which is not a characteristic often found in this group. The small flowers are produced singly, starting a strong yellow before paling with age. Perfect for a container as well as the edge of a border. Very healthy.

Oscar Peterson

HEIGHT *3ft (100cm)*   SPREAD *2ft (60cm)*
FLOWERING *Repeat*   TYPE *Shrub*   SCENT *None*
CULTIVAR *'AAC333'*   ZONES *3–8*

This belongs to the Easy Elegance group of roses, all of which combine great floriferousness with easy maintenance. 'Oscar Peterson' has large—up to 4in (10cm) wide—semi-double flowers that start a cream to soft yellow, but quickly become bright white. Bred in Canada, it is remarkably winter-hardy and healthy.

Grand Amore

HEIGHT *3½ft (1.1m)*   SPREAD *3ft (1m)*
FLOWERING *Repeat*   TYPE *Hybrid tea*   SCENT *Light*
CULTIVAR *'Korcoluma'*   ZONES *5–10*

One of the healthiest of red roses, it was given a prestigious award for health in Europe and named "Best Hybrid Tea" in Portland's Best Rose at the Portland Rose Festival in 2013. The flowers are classic hybrid tea, with the high-pointed center on long straight stems. Perfect for cutting and giving to a loved one or, indeed, anyone special.

'Chi'

'Oscar Peterson'

'Rise 'n' Shine'

'Grande Amore'

Roses for
the middle
of a border

Many rose varieties would suit the middle of a
border. I've focused on those around 4–5ft (1.2–1.5m)
tall, although, of course, you can adjust their height
by judicial pruning. They mix well with many
perennials of a similar height.

'Princess Alexandra of Kent'

Princess Alexandra of Kent

HEIGHT *4ft (1.2m)* SPREAD *4ft (1.2m)* FLOWERING *Repeat*
TYPE *David Austin English rose* SCENT *Strong tea*
CULTIVAR *'Ausmerchant'* ZONES *4–11*

A particularly beautiful variety with large, fragrant, very double blooms. The buds are pink with a hint of orange; when fully open, the flowers are a warm, glowing pink, paling a little toward the outside. With about 130 petals in each, the flowers have a very strong fragrance that is initially tea but becomes more lemony with age. The plant is bushy and slightly arching—a lovely rounded shrub, excellent by a path or in a pot (p.118), where the fragrance can easily be appreciated. It mixes very well with other plants, especially those with blue flowers.

Lady of Shalott

HEIGHT *5ft (1.5m)* SPREAD *4ft (1.2m)* FLOWERING *Repeat*
TYPE *David Austin English rose* SCENT *Medium to strong tea*
CULTIVAR *'Ausnyson'* ZONES *5–11*

An absolutely first-class variety that can be grown as a shrub or a climber. The flowers appear to be a rich apricot, although closer inspection shows that the insides of the petals are salmon-pink, whereas the outsides are more golden yellow. They are loosely double, meaning that the stamens are still accessible to bees. 'Lady of Shalott' flowers extremely freely, being hardly ever out of flower until late in the year. Tough and reliable, with slightly arching growth, it is best in a fairly large border, either with other roses or mixed in with perennials and shrubs.

Comte de Chambord

HEIGHT *4ft (1.2m)* SPREAD *3ft (1m)* FLOWERING *Repeat*
TYPE *Portland* SCENT *Strong old rose* ZONES *5–11*

'Comte de Chambord' is a particularly lovely old rose, that has the advantage of repeat-flowering and fairly upright growth. The flowers are a pure, rich pink, paling toward the outside. Its fragrance is one of the best of any rose, so should be planted where it is easy to access. It is not the healthiest of roses, but its other assets make up for this.

'Lady of Shalott'

'Comte de Chambord'

'Beverly Eleganza'

Beverly Eleganza

HEIGHT *4ft (1.2m)* SPREAD *3ft (1m)* FLOWERING *Repeat*
TYPE *Hybrid tea* SCENT *Strong fruity* CULTIVAR *'Korpauvio'*
ZONES *5–10*

A garden-worthy variety that combines a beautiful
flower with a strong fragrance. The young flowers have
the classic high-pointed center and retain their beauty
even when fully open. As they age, the mid-pink color
fades slightly, producing a lovely mix of shades. The
fruity fragrance is superb—citrus at first, with lychee
and white peach coming through later.

Bolero

HEIGHT *4ft (1.2m)* SPREAD *3ft (1m)*
FLOWERING *Repeat* TYPE *Floribunda*
SCENT *Strong fruity* CULTIVAR *'Meidelweis'* ZONES *5–10*

A pretty, healthy, and versatile rose. Traditionally,
floribundas don't have many petals and not too
much fragrance either, but 'Bolero' has plenty of both.
The fragrance is particularly appealing—strong and
fruity, with a hint of lemon verbena. With more than
100 petals, the blooms are full, making them look like
the old roses. A good choice for formal and informal
borders, and for cutting, too.

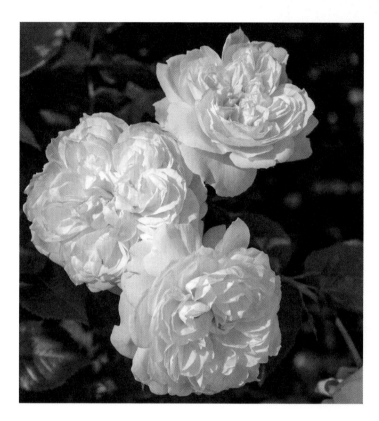

"The art of creating a truly beautiful border lies in identifying good partners that set one another off."

'Bolero'

Summer Romance

HEIGHT *4ft (1.2m)* SPREAD *3ft (1m)*
FLOWERING *Repeat* TYPE *Floribunda*
SCENT *Strong fruity* CULTIVAR *'Kortekcho'*
ZONES *5–10*

An extremely healthy, beautiful, and strongly fragrant rose, this variety won a prestigious award in Europe for its robust health. The medium-pink flowers are double, in the style of the old roses. Its height makes it perfect for the middle of the border, although plant it close enough to the path that the strong, delicious fragrance can be appreciated. The scent starts spicy and aniseed-like, but changes to fruity with age.

'Summer Romance'

Lion's Fairy Tale

HEIGHT *4ft (1.2m)* SPREAD *2½ft (75cm)* FLOWERING *Repeat*
TYPE *Floribunda* SCENT *Light to medium*
CULTIVAR *'Korvanaber'* ZONES *5–9*

With softly colored flowers and a neat, bushy habit,
'Champagne Moment' could be used in mixed borders
or in more formal planting arrangements. The blooms
are soft apricot in the center, paling to creamy white on
the outside, and are produced in large clusters. The
leaves are a dark, glossy green and particularly resistant
to disease. Also known as 'Lions-Rose'.

Gabriel Oak

HEIGHT *4ft (1.2m)* SPREAD *3ft (1m)*
FLOWERING *Repeat* TYPE *David Austin English rose*
SCENT *Strong fruity* CULTIVAR *'Auscrowd'*
ZONES *5–11*

A valuable variety with strongly colored, classically old
rose flowers that stand out in the middle of a border.
The blooms form a rosette and are a rich, deep
pink. They are held on a vigorous, relatively upright
shrub that would look lovely alongside shorter, softer-
pink flowers, be they roses or other plants. Lovely as
a cut flower, especially with its strong fruity fragrance.
A tough and reliable rose.

La Ville de Bruxelles

HEIGHT *5ft (1.5m)* SPREAD *4ft (1.2m)*
FLOWERING *Once* TYPE *Damask*
SCENT *Strong fruity old rose* ZONES *4–9*

A worthwhile variety, despite not repeat-flowering.
The large flowers are classically old rose in character,
the many pink petals arranged in a quartered effect with
a button eye in the center. They are set off by the large,
healthy, pale-green leaves. 'La Ville de Bruxelles' takes a
little time to mature and look its best, but it's worth
the wait.

Vanessa Bell

HEIGHT *4ft (1.2m)* SPREAD *3ft (1m)*
FLOWERING *Repeat* TYPE *David Austin English rose*
SCENT *Medium to strong tea* CULTIVAR *'Auseasel'*
ZONES *5–11*

A lovely soft-yellow variety, 'Vanessa Bell' is versatile,
tough, and reliable. The young buds are tinged with
pink, which soon disappears as they open into cup-
shaped, full-petaled flowers, deeper yellow in the
middle and creamy at the edge. It's a good idea to plant
this variety close to a path so that the blooms can be
easily accessed on a regular basis (they smell of green
tea, with touches of lemon and honey), and for ease of
cutting to bring into the house. It is bushy but upright
and so is an excellent choice for planting en masse,
although it is equally good in small groups or even
singly in a mixed border, where the soft yellow works
especially well with blues, purples, and lilacs.

'Lion's Fairy Tale'

'La Ville de Bruxelles'

'Gabriel Oak'

'Vanessa Bell'

Roses for the back of a border

Substantial roses that are 5ft (1.5m) or more
tall—and often the same across—are perfect
for a deep border that is backed by a wall,
fence, or hedge. They also look good as
specimens in a lawn or as part of a shrubbery.

'Francis Meilland'

Francis Meilland

HEIGHT *6ft (2m)*   SPREAD *3ft (1m)*   FLOWERING *Repeat*
TYPE *Hybrid tea*   SCENT *Strong fruity*   CULTIVAR *'Meltroni'*
ZONES *5–9*

A big rose in every respect! The flowers have the classic
hybrid-tea shape, but, at 5in (12cm) across, are bigger than
most. The color is a pleasing pale pink, with an above-average
number of petals, so when they go beyond the bud stage they
retain an attractive form. The fragrance is a delight—strong
and fruity, usually citrus. To cap it all, this rose is an award-
winner for its excellent health.

Rosa californica 'Plena'

HEIGHT *8ft (2.5m)*   SPREAD *6ft (2m)*   FLOWERING *Once*
TYPE *Species rose*   SCENT *Strong old rose*   ZONES *5–9*

A worthwhile rose of a character very different from modern
cultivars. It makes a large and magnificent shrub with great
quantities of relatively small, loosely double, mid-pink
flowers, and a delicious old rose fragrance. It will take a few
years to reach its full potential, but is well worth the wait. It
also looks superb in a wild setting in long grass.

The Lark Ascending

HEIGHT *6ft (2m)*   SPREAD *6ft (2m)*   FLOWERING *Repeat*
TYPE *David Austin English rose*   SCENT *Light tea/myrrh*
CULTIVAR *'Ausursula'*   ZONES *4–11*

A tough, reliable variety with fairly upright growth, 'The
Lark Ascending' is ideal as a backdrop to blue or purple
perennials such as catmints, salvias, campanulas, delphiniums,
or asters. The flowers are loosely semi-double and charming,
and they are produced freely from early summer until late
in the year. It is particularly healthy and winter hardy,
too—surprisingly, for a rose of this color and height.

Rosa californica 'Plena'

'The Lark Ascending'

Dee-Lish

HEIGHT *6ft (2m)*
SPREAD *3ft (1m)* FLOWERING *Repeat*
TYPE *Hybrid tea* SCENT *Strong fruity*
CULTIVAR *'Meiclusif'* ZONES *5–10*

The flowers on this tall, impressive hybrid tea have more petals than most varieties of the group, and so retain their beauty beyond the bud stage. Their color is mid-to-deep pink and fades little with age. With its excellent health and stature, it is perfect for the back of a border, although make sure it is easy to access, as the fragrance is strong and delicious—citrus with verbena. A welcome addition inside, too.

Cinderella

HEIGHT *5ft (1.5m)* SPREAD *3ft (1m)*
FLOWERING *Repeat* TYPE *Modern shrub* SCENT *Strong fruity*
CULTIVAR *'Korfobalt'* ZONES *5–9*

'Cinderella' has all the charm of the old roses, along with the advantages of the modern ones—good repeat-flowering and excellent health. The blooms are very double, with many petals beautifully arranged within an outer ring. The fragrance is strong and fruity—green apples with a hint of heliotrope. This rose is extremely healthy and has won a number of gold medals in competitions around Europe.

"With tall roses and other flowering shrubs, you can create a colorful, fragrance-filled shrubbery with year-round interest."

Thérèse Bugnet

HEIGHT *6ft (2m)*
SPREAD *4ft (1.2m)*
FLOWERING *Repeat*
TYPE *Rugosa hybrid*
SCENT *Strong old rose*
ZONES *3–9*

This is a little-known rose with many excellent qualities. Looking at it, one might never guess that it is a hybrid of the super-thorny rugosa roses, since it is almost completely thornless—although its rather rough leaves do suggest such a parentage. The flowers are very much in the character of a full-petaled old rose and have the fragrance to match. 'Thérèse Bugnet' is extremely healthy and winter hardy, although happy in Mediterranean climates as well.

Westerland

HEIGHT *6ft (2m)* SPREAD *5ft (1.5m)*
FLOWERING *Repeat*
TYPE *Modern shrub*
SCENT *Strong fruity*
CULTIVAR *'Korwest'* ZONES *5–10*

Some roses achieve fame quickly, and others, like 'Westerland', take time. The flowers are large, more than 4in (10cm) across, semi-double, and a real mix of vermillion, crimson, pink, yellow, and amber. While the unusual color blend sometimes makes finding suitable partners difficult, the overall effect is not harsh. The fragrance is strong and fruity, and the variety is very healthy. The flowers are followed by a good crop of long-lasting hips. Altogether an excellent variety.

Mother of Pearl

HEIGHT *5ft (150cm)*
SPREAD *2ft (60cm)*
FLOWERING *Repeat*
TYPE *Grandiflora* SCENT *Slight*
CULTIVAR *'Meiludere'* ZONES *5–10*

This rose performs well both in cool climates and those with hot, humid summers. 'Mother of Pearl' makes a free-flowering, tall, upright shrub perfect for the back of the border, where its soft, apricot-pink flowers are produced in great profusion. It needs little attention, aside from dead-heading and pruning in winter, and is lovely for cutting.

Penelope

HEIGHT *6ft (2m)* SPREAD *6ft (2m)* FLOWERING *Repeat*
TYPE *Hybrid musk* SCENT *Medium to strong fruity musk*
ZONES *6–11*

'Penelope' makes an excellent backdrop and also a fine free-standing shrub, its arching stems covered in flowers from the ground up. These are semi-double, opening slightly blush-pink but quickly turning white. If dead-headed, it repeats well; if not, it will produce a heavy crop of distinctive coral-pink hips. The fragrance is an interesting mix of fruitiness from the petals and musk from the gold stamens. This is a rose that is tolerant of some shade and poorer soil. In Mediterranean climates, it can easily become a climber.

Clair Matin

HEIGHT *8ft (2.5m) or 10ft (3m) as climber*
SPREAD *6ft (2m)* FLOWERING *Repeat*
TYPE *Modern shrub* SCENT *Light to medium sweet*
CULTIVAR *'Meimont'* ZONES *6–9*

'Clair Matin' is outstanding for the freedom with which it flowers from early summer until the cold stops it. The young buds are a soft peach, opening out to pale-pink, semi-double flowers, making it a good backdrop for all colors. Given all the effort it puts into producing so many flowers, it responds well to generous feeding and good conditions, although it copes well without such help. Can also be grown as a climber.

'Penelope'

'Clair Matin'

Roses for
mixed borders

These are roses of various heights that will look
superb planted alongside other plants. Perennials,
biennials, or annuals will set them off beautifully
and offer the opportunity of introducing blue into
your color scheme. A mixture of plants also
helps to keep roses healthy.

'Desdemona'

Desdemona

HEIGHT *3ft (1m)* SPREAD *3ft (1m)* FLOWERING *Repeat*
TYPE *David Austin English rose* SCENT *Strong fruity old rose*
CULTIVAR *'Auskindling'* ZONES *5–11*

Plants with pure white flowers can be difficult to integrate
into a garden, sometimes looking a bit hard and clinical. The
flowers of 'Desdemona', though, have a touch of blush in
them, especially when young, and will combine beautifully
with most other colors as long as they are not too strong.
This is a free-flowering variety producing masses of chalice-
shaped blooms. Though double, the flowers are not packed
with petals and so get a lovely interplay of light and shadow
within them. The fragrance is particularly delicious—a mix
of old rose with hints of almond blossom, cucumber, and
lemon zest, the latter sometimes coming very much to the
fore. A rose that is also excellent in a container (p.123).

Adobe Sunrise

HEIGHT *3ft (1m)* SPREAD *2ft (60cm)* FLOWERING *Repeat*
TYPE *Floribunda* SCENT *Slight* CULTIVAR *'Meipluvia'*
ZONES *5–10*

The name conjures up the color perfectly—a rich salmon-
orange that fades little with age. The flowers appear double
at first, the inner petals forming a hybrid-tea-type flower that
opens to reveal a generous bunch of stamens. The variety
makes a neat, compact bush that fits nicely in a narrow
border. Excellent, too, in a container.

Eustacia Vye

HEIGHT *4ft (1.2m)* SPREAD *3ft (1m)* FLOWERING *Repeat*
TYPE *David Austin English rose* SCENT *Strong fruity*
CULTIVAR *'Ausegdon'* ZONES *5–11*

The soft pink and apricot coloring of 'Eustacia Vye' makes it
an easy variety to incorporate in a mixed border. Its growth
is quite upright, perfect behind something short such
as *Erigeron karvinskianus*, *Nepeta*, or pinks (*Dianthus*), but
make sure you can reach the flowers to smell their strong,
fruity fragrance. It is a very healthy variety and repeat-flowers
well; it can even be used as a short climber (p.174).

'Adobe Sunrise'

'Eustacia Vye'

'Felicia'

'Madame Hardy'

Madame Hardy

HEIGHT *5ft (1.5m) or 8ft (2.5m) as climber*
SPREAD *4ft (1.2m)* FLOWERING *Once*
TYPE *Damask* SCENT *Strong old rose* ZONES *5–9*

One of the most beautiful of the old roses and one of the easiest to recognize. 'Madame Hardy' is one of the very few good white old roses, and its little green eye makes it simplet to identify. The long, green, leafy sepals are characteristic, too. The blooms are a perfectly formed rosette and deliciously fragrant. If lightly pruned, it can get fairly tall and even make a lovely climber.

Felicia

HEIGHT *5ft (1.5m) or 8ft (2.5m) as climber* SPREAD *5ft (1.5m)*
FLOWERING *Repeat* TYPE *Hybrid musk* SCENT *Medium to
strong fruity musk* ZONES *6–11*

One of the best hybrid musks, 'Felicia' flowers freely and is
very healthy. The flowers are loosely double with petals that
are rose-pink above and apricot below, giving an overall
impression of a silvery salmon-pink. In the fall, the color is
richer and the flowers are produced in bigger clusters. If
pruned lightly, it can get quite big, and in warmer climates
become a climber. Lovely mixed with other flowers.

Lichfield Angel

HEIGHT *4ft (1.2m)* SPREAD *4ft (1.2m)*
FLOWERING *Repeat* TYPE *David Austin English rose*
SCENT *Light musk* CULTIVAR *'Ausrelate'* ZONES *5–11*

A particularly free-flowering variety with rather lax, arching
growth that looks superb with the many perennials of a
similar habit. The flowers start a pale peachy pink, but when
fully open are creamy white in the form of a loose rosette,
the outer petals eventually reflexing back. Looks lovely with
catmint in front of it and has the advantage of being
practically thornless. Also makes a fine hedge.

The Lady Gardener

HEIGHT *4ft (1.2m)* SPREAD *4ft (1.2m)*
FLOWERING *Repeat* TYPE *David Austin English rose*
SCENT *Strong tea* CULTIVAR *'Ausbrass'* ZONES *5–11*

It is easy to find good bedfellows for roses with apricot
flowers. The obvious ones are the purples of plants such as
salvias, but by trying flowers of other colors you will soon
find that many work well. With its strong, bushy growth
even one plant of 'The Lady Gardener' can make a statement
(p.118), although a group of three planted closely together
has an even better effect. It has a lovely fragrance, essentially
tea with hints of cedarwood and vanilla.

'Lichfield Angel'

'The Lady Gardener'

Burgundy Iceberg

HEIGHT *4ft (1.2m)* SPREAD *3ft (1m)*
FLOWERING *Repeat* TYPE *Floribunda*
SCENT *Light honey* CULTIVAR *'Prose'*
ZONES *6–9*

'Burgundy Iceberg', like the popular 'Iceberg' it sported from, is an amazing flowering machine, especially in warm climates. For many years, except for it sporting to a climber, 'Iceberg' stayed stable, until two color sports appeared— 'Brilliant Pink' and 'Burgundy'. As the name suggests, the color is a purple-red burgundy; the cooler the weather, the deeper the shade. An easy rose to mix with other plants, especially in shades of pink, it is excellent as a tree rose. The stems are nearly thornless.

Intrigue

HEIGHT *2½ft (75cm)* SPREAD *3ft (1m)*
FLOWERING *Repeat* TYPE *Floribunda*
SCENT *Strong citrus* CULTIVAR *'Jacum'*
ZONES *6–9*

'Intrigue' dates to the early 1980s, but, unlike many roses bred at that time, it is still an excellent, worthwhile variety. The flowers are a wonderful reddish-purple color that turns almost bluish with age. Its fragrance is delicious, strong, and citrusy. Good for borders of all sizes.

Orchid Romance

HEIGHT *4½ft (1.4m)*
SPREAD *3ft (1m)*
FLOWERING *Repeat*
TYPE *Floribunda* SCENT *Strong citrus*
CULTIVAR *'Radprov'* ZONES *5–10*

This is a very different looking rose from 'Knock Out', although both were bred by Bill Radler. The flowers resemble those of an old rose, with each bloom having 80 to 90 petals and a strong citrus fragrance. The color varies from mid-to-dark pink, with lavender undertones. A healthy variety that is easy to look after.

The Shepherdess

HEIGHT *4ft (1.2m)*
SPREAD *3ft (1m)*
FLOWERING *Repeat*
TYPE *David Austin English rose*
SCENT *Medium fruity*
CULTIVAR *'Austwist'* ZONES *5–11*

In any border it is important to have a balance of plants that demand attention and those that, while also beautiful and worthwhile, work well in the background. 'The Shepherdess' is a perfect example of such a variety. The blooms are a soft apricot, veering toward pink in some weathers, and the shape a deep cup with the stamens showing as the flower ages. It has a delicious fruity fragrance with hints of lemon.

Ipsilanté

HEIGHT *5ft (1.5m)* SPREAD *4ft (1.2m)*
FLOWERING *Once* TYPE *Gallica*
SCENT *Strong old rose* ZONES *4–8*

A classic and very lovely gallica with fragrant, rich-pink flowers. It is also spelled 'Ypsilanté'. The arrangement of petals gives a roughly quartered effect, with a little green eye sometimes visible in the center. The stems are a bit lax and floppy, which means the flowers intermingle with those of their neighbors, creating beautiful color combinations.

Lavender Lassie

HEIGHT *6ft (2m)* SPREAD *4ft (1.2m)*
FLOWERING *Repeat* TYPE *Hybrid musk*
SCENT *Strong sweet*
ZONES *6–11*

'Lavender Lassie' is, unfortunately, often overlooked. It has an unassuming character, but is so beautiful and undemanding. For a rose introduced in 1960, when hybrid teas and floribundas were at their maximum popularity, this was something different. The flowers are double, old-roselike, and beautifully scented. The color is slightly lavender, paling nicely with age. It copes well with shade, and with that, the pink hardly pales at all. In cooler climates, it makes a wonderful bushy shrub; in warmer ones, it becomes a lovely climber of about 10ft (3m).

Princess Anne

HEIGHT *4ft (1.2m)* SPREAD *4ft (1.2m)*
FLOWERING *Repeat* TYPE *David Austin English rose*
SCENT *Medium tea* CULTIVAR *'Auskitchen'* ZONES *5–11*

This is a variety that will stand out in a border with its big, bold flowers, the color fading as it ages from a really rich, almost red-pink to mid-pink. It is a particularly tough and reliable rose that will cope well with less than ideal conditions and fit in perfectly with a wide range of other plants, as long as they are not planted so close that they compete with it for water and nutrients. It associates well with softer colors like the silver leaves of *Stachys byzantina* and *Artemisia* 'Powis Castle' as well as the lilac or lavender flowers of catmint, lavender, and salvia. The fragrance is variable, sometimes strong, and other times not.

Summer Memories

HEIGHT *4ft (1.2m)* SPREAD *2ft (60cm)*
FLOWERING *Repeat* TYPE *Modern shrub*
SCENT *Light* CULTIVAR *'Koruteli'* ZONES *5–9*

A rose with the classic full-petaled flowers of the old roses. Good old roses with pure or creamy white flowers are difficult to find, so this is a useful alternative, especially as it has excellent disease resistance. An easy rose to mix into the middle of a border with shorter plants in front and (if space allows) taller ones behind.

'Summer Memories'

'Princess Anne' (mid-pink rose, right)

'Great Maiden's Blush'

Great Maiden's Blush

HEIGHT *6ft (2m)* SPREAD *4ft (1.2m)* FLOWERING *Once*
TYPE *Alba* SCENT *Strong old rose* ZONES *4–9*

This is one of the most beautiful of the old roses, and
one of the oldest, too, dating back to around 1550 or
earlier. It has many other names, including 'Cuisse
de Nymphe'. It is obviously a great survivor and will
think nothing of competition from other plants or lack
of care. The soft pink flowers, fading to white, are easy
to integrate into a mixed border. Plant it where the
blooms will be accessible so that their wonderful
fragrance can be easily and regularly appreciated.

Garden Delight

HEIGHT *4ft (1.2m)* SPREAD *3ft (1m)*
FLOWERING *Repeat* TYPE *Floribunda* SCENT *Medium*
CULTIVAR *'Korgohowa'* ZONES *5–9*

If you want a real standout, then here is a strong contender. Unlike a standard floribunda, the flowers on this rose are large—with the high-pointed center more typical of hybrid teas—and very full-petaled. The center of the flower is a rich yellow, while the outside varies from pink to red, the shade dependant on the weather: the sunnier it is, the deeper the color. A very healthy rose.

Olivia Rose Austin

HEIGHT *4ft (1.2m)* SPREAD *3ft (1m)*
FLOWERING *Repeat* TYPE *David Austin English rose*
SCENT *Light to medium fruity* CULTIVAR *'Ausmixture'*
ZONES *5–11*

This is an outstanding rose both for the number of flowers it produces and for its health. It starts flowering a good two to three weeks before most other roses and then repeats quickly and carries on until late in the year. The flowers open to shallow cups of mid-pink, set off nicely by the slightly gray tinge in the foliage. It can be used in many different ways in the garden, but it is perhaps best suited to mixing in with other plants. Different shades of pink will look lovely next to it, as will contrasting purples, blues, and even soft yellows.

Rosa gallica var. *officinalis*

HEIGHT *4ft (1.2m)* SPREAD *3ft (1m)*
FLOWERING *Once* TYPE *Gallica*
SCENT *Strong old rose* ZONES *4–8*

Also known as the apothecary's rose and the red rose of Lancaster, this may well be the oldest of the old roses to be found in gardens today. Grown in huge quantities in many parts of Europe, especially in the French town of Provins, it has long been used for culinary, medicinal, and cosmetic purposes. The flowers are quite large, magenta-pink and semi-double, with contrasting yellow stamens. It is particularly tough and will not be too troubled by competition from invading perennials. Hips follow the flowers, although they are a dull red.

Tupelo Honey

HEIGHT *4ft (1.2m)* SPREAD *3ft (1m)* FLOWERING *Repeat*
TYPE *Floribunda* SCENT *Medium* CULTIVAR *'Korflusamea'*
ZONES *5–9*

An ideal variety for mixing into the cottage garden. Certain yellow roses can be harsh and don't mix well, but Tupelo Honey contains some butterscotch, which makes it much easier to integrate. Plus, the flowers are full-petaled, like the old roses. It is not too vigorous, so perfect for a medium-sized border. Makes a pretty palette with purple- and lavender-colored flowers.

'Garden Delight'

Rosa gallica var. officinalis

'Olivia Rose Austin'

'Tupelo Honey'

Roses for containers

A rose in a container is a wonderful way of bringing color and perfume to a patio, deck, balcony, or any area where it is not possible to plant anything in the ground. The best varieties are small, rounded, and have a delicious fragrance.

The Lady Gardener

HEIGHT *4ft (1.2m)* SPREAD *4ft (1.2m)*
FLOWERING *Repeat* TYPE *David Austin English rose*
SCENT *Strong tea* CULTIVAR *'Ausbrass'* ZONES *5–11*

With its rather upright, bushy growth, 'The Lady Gardener' is a substantial and beautiful rose for a pot. The large apricot flowers have the most delicious tea fragrance with hints of cedarwood and vanilla. Placing the container against a light-colored wall will help to set the flowers off and encourage earlier flowering. A healthy rose that will repeat-flower well.

Princess Alexandra of Kent

HEIGHT *4ft (1.2m)* SPREAD *4ft (1.2m)*
FLOWERING *Repeat* TYPE *David Austin English rose*
SCENT *Strong tea and fruit* CULTIVAR *'Ausmerchant'*
ZONES *5–11*

The large rich-pink flowers of 'Princess Alexandra of Kent' make a statement in a pot. Its strong tea fragrance with a lemon finish, its toughness, and its reliability are also ideal characteristics for a container-grown rose. In the border (p.97), it is a fairly upright, bushy plant, but in a pot, with more light around the base, it becomes more rounded and produces flowers lower down.

'The Lady Gardener'

'Princess Alexandra of Kent'

Herzogin Christiana

HEIGHT *2½ft (75cm)*
SPREAD *1½ft (45cm)*
FLOWERING *Repeat*
TYPE *Floribunda*
SCENT *Strong fruit*
CULTIVAR *'Korgeowim'*
ZONES *5–9*

This is a neat, fairly upright variety, with soft-pink flowers that would look pretty in a blue-glazed pot. The blooms are a little unusual, being very rounded and only opening up partially. They are soft-pink in the middle and more of a creamy white on the outer petals. The fruity fragrance is particularly strong—a lovely mix of lemon, raspberries, and apple.

Easy Does It

HEIGHT *3ft (1m)* SPREAD *3ft (1m)*
FLOWERING *Repeat* TYPE *Floribunda*
SCENT *Medium fruity*
CULTIVAR *'Harpageant'*
ZONES *6–10*

This distinctive rose has richly colored petals ending in scalloped edges. An initial deep orange-apricot, 'Easy Does It' fades gradually to peachy-apricot. It flowers freely and, even though it was bred by Harkness in the UK, it is well-suited to hot, dry climates as well as cooler, wetter ones.

Bliss Parfuma

HEIGHT *3ft (100cm)*
SPREAD *2½ft (75cm)*
FLOWERING *Repeat*
TYPE *Hybrid tea* SCENT *Strong fruity*
CULTIVAR *'Kormarzau'* ZONES *5–10*

The flowers start in the hybrid tea shape, but are at their most beautiful when fully open—it is then that the more than 100 petals are exposed in a perfect old rose arrangement. As one might expect, the fragrance is very strong—deliciously fruity. An award-winner, it is extremely healthy. This versatile variety is excellent for a mixed border, containers, and for bringing into the house.

Joie de Vivre

HEIGHT *2ft (60cm)*
SPREAD *1½ft (45cm)*
FLOWERING *Repeat*
TYPE *Floribunda* SCENT *Light*
CULTIVAR *'Korfloci01'*
ZONES *6–9*

A compact and extremely healthy variety perfect for a smaller pot in a more confined area. The pretty blooms are in the style of an old rose, with many petals arranged in a rosette, the color being a soft apricot-pink, paling toward the outside. An award-winning, extremely healthy rose, also known as 'Garden of Roses'.

First Crush

HEIGHT *3ft (100cm)*
SPREAD *2½ft (75cm)*
FLOWERING *Repeat*
TYPE *Floribunda* SCENT *Strong fruity*
CULTIVAR *'Kormaccap'* ZONES *5–11*

This is an ideal rose for a container. The growth is compact, so easy to manage, and fits neatly into a medium-sized pot. It has a superb fresh, fruity fragrance, perfect for placing close to seats. And, importantly, its beautiful, full-petaled, soft-colored flowers associate well with other plants, whether in a pot or in the garden. An extremely healthy variety.

"A pot-grown rose becomes a focal point—especially so if it's a small variety that might otherwise get lost in a mixed bed."

'South Africa'

'Desdemona'

South Africa

HEIGHT *3ft (1m)*   SPREAD *3ft (1m)*   FLOWERING *Repeat*
TYPE *Floribunda*   SCENT *Medium sweet*   CULTIVAR *'Korberbeni'*
ZONES *5–10*

As its name suggests, this rose has rich golden-yellow flowers set off by dark-green leaves. At the bud stage, the flowers have the classic high-pointed center of a hybrid tea, but then open up to reveal gold stamens. 'Golden Beauty' is extremely healthy (it is a winner of many awards) and flourishes in the hot conditions often found on a patio, terrace, or balcony.

Desdemona

HEIGHT *3ft (1m)*   SPREAD *3ft (1m)*   FLOWERING *Repeat*
TYPE *David Austin English rose*   SCENT *Strong fruity old rose*
CULTIVAR *'Auskindling'*   ZONES *5–11*

With its strong, delicious fragrance and excellent freedom of flowering, 'Desdemona' is a good choice for containers. It is not too tall or vigorous and will be happy in a medium-sized pot, although, as with all roses in containers, it is important to keep it well watered to encourage maximum flowering. The soft creamy white flowers look good in a blue pot.

Marie Pavié

HEIGHT *2ft (60cm)*   SPREAD *2½ft (75cm)*   FLOWERING *Repeat*
TYPE *Polyantha*   SCENT *Strong musk*   ZONES *5–11*

'Marie Pavié' (also spelled 'Pavič') was introduced toward the end of the 19th century and remains a good rose, especially in containers. The scent is musky, the type that floats on the air, and so can be enjoyed even if sitting some distance away. The soft-pink flowers, fading to white, are produced almost ceaselessly from summer to fall.

'Marie Pavié'

Roses for tight spaces

These roses are all short in stature or narrow in width, to
fit into small gardens and odd gaps. The flowers are small
or medium-sized, and variable in petal count and form, ranging
from single to very double—just like an old rose. They are
also good choices for smaller containers.

'Jolie Veranda'

Jolie Veranda

HEIGHT *2½ft (75cm)* SPREAD *2ft (60cm)*
FLOWERING *Repeat* TYPE *Shrub* SCENT *Light*
CULTIVAR *'Korfloci54'* ZONES *5–11*

A cheerfully colored rose that copes well with difficult situations. The flowers are medium-sized and a bright salmon-pink that doesn't fade. The petals drop cleanly— important to consider when choosing a rose for the garden, especially when planting one that flowers as continuously as this one does. A tough, reliable rose that looks most effective with blue or purple flowers.

Julia Child

HEIGHT *3ft (1m)* SPREAD *2ft (60cm)* FLOWERING *Repeat*
TYPE *Floribunda* SCENT *Medium to strong myrrh*
CULTIVAR *'Wekvossutono'* ZONES *5–9*

Since its introduction in 2004, this has become a firm favorite in many parts of the world, a reflection not only of its qualities but also of its ability to flourish in different climates. The flowers are a warm golden-yellow, paling with age to creamy white. It has a good myrrh fragrance, although some perceive it as more like aniseed. It is particularly free-flowering and healthy. An excellent choice for a small border, on its own, or planted as a group of two or three or more, if space allows. Also good in more formal bedding areas.

Pretty Polly Lavender

HEIGHT *1½ft (45cm)* SPREAD *2ft (60cm)*
FLOWERING *Repeat* TYPE *Polyantha* SCENT *Light*
CULTIVAR *'Zlepolthree'* ZONES *4–10*

A compact rose perfect for tight spots, be they in a border or container. It is remarkably winter-hardy, but at the same time happy to grow in warmer climates. The flowers are small, only a touch over an inch across, but full of narrow petals, which give it a charming appearance. Pale lavender color. Very healthy.

'Julia Child'

'Pretty Polly Lavender'

Katharina Zeimet

HEIGHT *3ft (1m)* SPREAD *2½ft (75cm)*
FLOWERING *Repeat* TYPE *Dwarf Polyantha*
SCENT *Medium sweet* ZONES *5–11*

This is one of the most continuous-flowering of all roses. While the individual flowers are not particularly shapely, they are fragrant, and the sheer quantity, the long flowering period, and the way they are produced in large clusters make up for this. If lightly pruned or grown in warm climates, it can grow substantially taller than normal. Winter-hardy.

Roxy

HEIGHT *2ft (60cm)* SPREAD *1ft (30cm)*
FLOWERING *Repeat* TYPE *Miniature* SCENT *None*
CULTIVAR *'Korsineo'* ZONES *5–9*

A truly miniature rose, even though the flowers look like those of the old roses, with their petals beautifully arranged in a rosette. A bright, unfading pink that sometimes leans toward purple, the color is brighter than you would find in an old rose. Free-flowering and extremely healthy, too.

Flamingo Kolorscape

HEIGHT *3ft (1m)* SPREAD *2ft (60cm)*
FLOWERING *Repeat* TYPE *Shrub* SCENT *Very light*
CULTIVAR *'Korhopiko'* ZONES *5–11*

A vibrantly colored rose that brightens any position in the garden. The semi-double flowers are brilliant pink, with the hint of a white eye, the color not fading at all. They are produced continuously from first flower to late in the year, and, luckily, the petals drop cleanly. An award-winner for extreme good health.

Lemon Fizz

HEIGHT *2½ft (75cm)* SPREAD *2ft (60cm)*
FLOWERING *Repeat* TYPE *Modern shrub* SCENT *Light*
CULTIVAR *'Korfizzlem'* ZONES *5–11*

A very useful rose that, with its compact growth, is excellent for brightening the corners of the garden, patio, or balcony. The unfading, bright-yellow flowers are produced continuously and, with the stamens fully exposed, are much loved by bees. Extremely healthy and suitable for planting in both the ground and in pots.

'Katharina Zeimet'

'Flamingo Kolorscape'

'Roxy'

'Lemon Fizz'

'Cream Veranda'

'Diamond Eyes'

Cream Veranda

HEIGHT *2½ft (75cm)* SPREAD *2ft (60cm)*
FLOWERING *Repeat* TYPE *Floribunda*
SCENT *Light to medium* CULTIVAR *'Korfloci01'*
ZONES *5–11*

A compact, healthy variety perfect for a tight spot or a small pot. The pretty blooms are in the style of the old roses, with the many petals arranged in a rosette. The color is a soft apricot-pink, paling toward the outside. Award winner given only to the healthiest of roses.

Diamond Eyes

HEIGHT *1½ft (45cm)* SPREAD *1ft (30cm)*
FLOWERING *Repeat* TYPE *Miniature* SCENT *Strong and clovelike* CULTIVAR *'Wekwibypur'* ZONES *4–10*

The flowers of 'Diamond Eyes' are much like the deep-purple flowers of the big, once-flowering rambler 'Violette'. Aside from that, the varieties are completely different! A miniature that grows to 12–18in (30–45cm) tall, 'Diamond Eyes' repeat-flowers well. The flowers are a deep purple, with a striking white eye, and the fragrance is strong and clovelike. A lovely little rose for a container, raised bed, windowsill, or narrow border.

Pretty Polly White

HEIGHT *3ft (1m)* SPREAD *3ft (1m)*
FLOWERING *Repeat* TYPE *Polyantha*
SCENT *Very light* CULTIVAR *'Zlepoltwo'* ZONES *4–10*

A charming, but tough rose. Unlike 'Pretty Polly Lavender' (p.125), the flowers of this variety are semi-double, showing off their bright-yellow bunch of stamens. They are also a bit smaller and are produced continuously until late in the year. It can withstand cold winters as well as thrive in hot summers. A third variety in this series—'Pretty Polly Pink'—has the same characteristics.

"Fewer colors work especially well in tight spaces: for best effects, try using an edited color palette when designing a border for a small garden."

'Pretty Polly White'

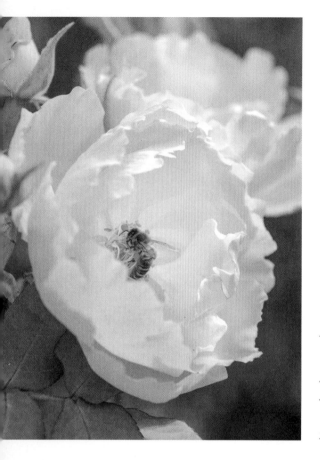

'Comte de Champagne'

Roses for wildlife

Roses of all sizes and types can be excellent for encouraging wildlife into your garden. The varieties showcased here all have single or semi-double flowers, to encourage as many beneficial insects into the garden as possible. Many also produce hips, a valuable food source during the winter months, while their stems offer cover for birds and small mammals.

Rosa laevigata

Comte de Champagne

HEIGHT *4ft (1.2m)* SPREAD *4ft (1.2m)* FLOWERING *Repeat*
TYPE *David Austin English rose* SCENT *Light to medium musk*
CULTIVAR *'Ausufo'* ZONES *5–11*

'Comte de Champagne' has simple but charming semi-double
flowers, which, with their large number of stamens, are most
attractive to bees. The apricot young flowers and soft
creamy-yellow older ones make for a lovely mix of different
shades, making it an easy rose to incorporate into a border.

Rosa laevigata

HEIGHT *5ft (1.5m) as a shrub or 15ft (4.5m) as a climber*
SPREAD *10ft (3m) as a shrub or 10ft (3m) as a climber*
FLOWERING *Single* TYPE *Wild rose* SCENT *Strong fruity*
ZONES *7–11*

R. laevigata is native to Southern China and Vietnam. It has
since naturalized in the American South and is the state
flower of Georgia; it is also known as the 'Cherokee Rose'.
The five-petaled flowers are pure white and large, about
3.5in (9in) across, and strongly scented. This rose does not
repeat-flower, but it does set a magnificent crop of large
orange hips. Excellent for naturalizing in warm areas, it can
be grown as a mounding shrub or for clambering into trees.
A healthy rose that needs no maintenance, it should not be
planted too close to a path.

Summer Wine

HEIGHT *12ft (3.6m)* SPREAD *6ft (2m)* FLOWERING *Repeat*
TYPE *Climber* SCENT *Medium* CULTIVAR *'Korizont'*
ZONES *5–9*

'Summer Wine' is valuable for bees at flowering time and
birds in fall and early winter. The flowers are medium to
large and officially semi-double, but, with only eight to 10
petals, look more single. The buds are bright coral, opening
to a soft salmon-pink with a yellow center. Standing out
from the center are the stamens, with crimson filaments and
yellow anthers. The rose will repeat-flower, however, if the
large, rounded, orange hips are wanted, leave some of the
dead flowers. Grown as a climber or, with harder pruning,
kept as a large shrub. A pretty, tough rose.

'Summer Wine'

Morning Mist

HEIGHT *6ft (2m)* SPREAD *5ft (1.5m)*
FLOWERING *Repeat* TYPE *David Austin English rose*
SCENT *Light musk* CULTIVAR *'Ausfire'* ZONES *5–9*

A large and eye-catching rose for the back of the border or a wilder area. The flowers are single and are a strong shade of coral pink, with a large boss of stamens with red filaments. While the color might sound a little tricky, it is, in fact, not too bright and not difficult to find good partners for. The flowers are followed by large orange hips that last right through the winter.

Rosa × richardii

HEIGHT *3ft (1m)* SPREAD *4ft (1.2m)*
FLOWERING *Single* TYPE *Species hybrid*
SCENT *Light musk* ZONES *6–9*

The origin of this rose (also known as *R. sancta*) is a real mystery. Stems with identical blooms were found in Egyptian tombs dating as far back as 200 CE, but there is no certain history of it in cultivation before 1890. Whatever its history, it is a beautiful rose, with large single species-like flowers that start soft pink, paling to blush. The petals are slightly crumpled, not unlike those of the rock rose (*Cistus*). It may be a cross between *R. gallica* and *R. arvensis*, the first supplying its large flowers and the second its elegant arching growth. Unfortunately, it produces hardly any hips, but it is attractive to insects. It is tough, growing well even in difficult positions.

Polyantha Grandiflora

HEIGHT *23ft (7m)* SPREAD *16ft (5m)*
FLOWERING *Once* TYPE *Rambler*
SCENT *Strong musk* ZONES *6–9*

This is one of the best roses for bees—when it's in flower, the buzzing can be heard from some distance away. The individual blooms are a little larger than those of most wild roses and slightly on the creamy side of white. They have a strong and delicious musky fragrance that can be smelled almost before the rose is seen. At close quarters, it is more clovelike. Great quantities of small red hips are produced that will last through the winter, unless taken by the birds. The leaves too are attractive—glossy and with a crimson midrib. An excellent choice for growing up a tree or somewhere where it can be allowed to spread at will. Also excellent for arrangements, whether in summer with the flowers or winter with the hips.

Topolina

HEIGHT *1½ft (45cm)* SPREAD *2ft (60cm)*
FLOWERING *Repeat* TYPE *Modern shrub*
SCENT *Light* CULTIVAR *'Korpifleu'* ZONES *5–9*

The great mass of stamens in the middle of each flower of 'Topolina' is hugely attractive to bees and other insects. The blooms, which are produced very freely, are single and a fairly bright pink, with a soft yellow eye. The rose is award-winning and extremely healthy. A good choice for the edge of a path or as ground cover.

'Morning Mist'

'Polyantha Grandiflora'

Rosa x richardii

'Topolina'

"While roses lack nectar, their pollen is highly nutritious, providing a valuable food source to bees, hoverflies, beetles, and other insects."

Fire Opal Kolorscape

HEIGHT *2½ft (75cm)*   SPREAD *1½ft (45cm)*
FLOWERING *Repeat*   TYPE *Floribunda*   SCENT *Slight*
CULTIVAR *'Korumneza'*   ZONES *5–9*

The flowers of this rose change color according to their age and the weather. They are surprisingly large, about 4in (10cm) across, and, with only 10 to 15 petals, the large bunch of stamens is exposed, attracting bees. The color varies from to coral to cream, giving a lovely mix at any one time. Very healthy and winter-hardy.

'Fire Opal Kolorscape'

'Fortuna' (shown in foreground with *Hosta* 'Cripula')

Fortuna

HEIGHT *2ft (60cm)*   SPREAD *1½ft (45cm)*
FLOWERING *Repeat*   TYPE *Modern shrub*
SCENT *Light*   CULTIVAR *'Koratomi'*   ZONES *6–9*

A pretty, softly colored variety with masses of flowers that are particularly attractive to pollinators. The salmon-pink flowers pale to blush, giving a lovely mix of colors. It has a fairly bushy, upright habit that is easy to mix in with other plants, especially those with blue, lilac, or purple flowers. Very healthy.

The Lady's Blush

HEIGHT *4ft (1.2m)*   SPREAD *3ft (1m)*
FLOWERING *Repeat*   TYPE *David Austin English rose*
SCENT *Light*   CULTIVAR *'Ausoscar'*   ZONES *5–11*

A medium-sized shrub, 'The Lady's Blush' produces great quantities of semi-double flowers that are loved by bees. They are a soft mid-pink with a white eye and a central ring of red where the stamens are attached. If not dead-headed, hips will follow the flowers. A tough and reliable rose for the middle of a border or in a wilder area.

'The Lady's Blush'

Roses for wild areas

The species roses and their near relatives are perfect for wilder parts of the garden, fitting especially well into meadow and prairie-style planting. They have beautiful flowers and hips, and sometimes fall leaf color, too. Some are quite compact, while others—given the chance—will scramble up into trees. Most are tolerant of poorer soils.

Rosa hugonis

Rosa hugonis

HEIGHT *8ft (2.5m)*   SPREAD *6ft (2m)*
FLOWERING *Once*   TYPE *Species rose*
SCENT *Light*   ZONES *5–9*

This is perhaps the most beautiful of all the yellow wild roses, and indeed of all the species. The flowers are a soft primrose-yellow with a bunch of golden yellow stamens in the center, which bees are very attracted to. The foliage is tiny and fernlike. *Rosa hugonis* will take a few years to reach maturity, during which time it shouldn't be pruned, so it is important to make sure it has the space to reach its full potential.

Rosa canina

HEIGHT *10ft (3m)*   SPREAD *8ft (2.5m)*
FLOWERING *Once*   TYPE *Species rose*
SCENT *Light*   ZONES *3–9*

This is the familiar dog rose, native to the British Isles and much of Europe, with simple five-petaled flowers that somehow are so beautiful. Their color is usually a soft rose-pink, but varies from deep pink to almost white. It is a vigorous rose that can easily scramble high up into a tree, so its positioning needs to be carefully considered. It will still flower freely even if planted in a hedge and trimmed regularly. The flowers are followed by long, oval, vermillion hips. There are a few hybrids of *Rosa canina*, the outstanding one being *R. × hibernica*, which produces a fine crop of extremely long-lasting, dark-red hips.

Rosa canina

Complicata

HEIGHT *5ft (1.5m) or 10ft (3m) as climber*
SPREAD *6ft (2m)* FLOWERING *Once*
TYPE *Species hybrid* SCENT *Light* *4–9*

This is not a true species rose but a hybrid between *Rosa gallica* and *R. canina*. The large flowers (5in/13cm across) are rose-pink with a white center and have a large clump of stamens. As a shrub, it has quite vigorous and rather lax growth, which encourages a profusion of flowers. It also makes an attractive climber. The flowers are followed by large red hips. It looks beautiful planted among long grass and oxeye daisies.

Rosa virginiana

HEIGHT *5ft (1.5m)* SPREAD *4ft (1.2m)* FLOWERING *Once*
TYPE *Species rose* SCENT *Medium to strong* ZONES *3–9*

Unlike many species roses, *Rosa virginiana* doesn't grow too big and so works well in medium-sized gardens. The cerise-pink flowers start to appear fairly late, after midsummer, but continue for a good six weeks. By October, the shiny round hips color up to a bright red and can stay on until the following spring. The leaves too are attractive, being brightly colored in spring and then again later in the year, when a whole range of glorious autumnal tints appears. The stems are red-brown in winter and relatively thornless. In addition, this rose is extremely tough and will grow well in both shade and poor soil.

Rosa woodsii 'Mountain Rose'

HEIGHT *6ft (2m)* SPREAD *5ft (1.5m)*
FLOWERING *Single* TYPE *Wild rose* SCENT *Strong*
ZONES *2–9*

Rosa woodsii is native to North America, from Alaska to New Mexico, with most found in Montana and Alberta, Canada, often in wetlands. Depending on soil quality and climate, it can be as short as 2–3ft (60–100cm), although in garden situations it easily reaches 6ft (2m). It can sucker, too, depending on the planting site. The single flowers are a range of pure pinks, based on where the seed was collected. A crop of long-lasting, medium-sized, rounded, red hips follows. Good fall color on the leaves.

Rosa nutkana

HEIGHT *6ft (2m)* SPREAD *4ft (1.2m)* FLOWERING *Once*
TYPE *Species rose* SCENT *Light* ZONES *3–8*

While most wild roses will grow into very large shrubs, *Rosa nutkana* is rather smaller and so easier to fit in. The flowers are lilac-pink, slightly darker in the middle, which creates an effective background for the golden yellow stamens. The round orange-red hips are very persistent. An easy and trouble-free rose to grow.

'Complicata'

Rosa woodsii 'Mountain Rose'

Rosa virginiana

Rosa nutkana

'Darlow's Enigma'

Rosa palustris

Rosa palustris

HEIGHT *4ft (1.2m)* SPREAD *4ft (1.2m)*
FLOWERING *Once* TYPE *Species rose*
SCENT *Light to medium* ZONES *3–9*

In its native North America, *Rosa palustris* goes by the common name 'Swamp Rose,' although it grows just as happily, if not better, in poor, sandy soils. The flowers start late, continuing well into late summer, and are a pure mid-pink. They are larger than those of most species roses, especially the North American ones. *Rosa palustris* does produce hips, although they are not particularly large or noticeable. It's a perfect rose for a wild area, where it will sucker freely.

Darlow's Enigma

HEIGHT *12ft (3.6m)* SPREAD *6ft (2m)*
FLOWERING *Repeat* TYPE *Hybrid musk rambler*
SCENT *Medium to strong* ZONES *4–10*

This outstanding rose, discovered by Mike Darlow in 1993, is a favorite of bees. A free-flowering rose, it is more or less continuous, especially in warmer climates. The small, white, single, or slightly semi-double flowers are produced in big bunches, followed in fall by great quantities of small red hips. Grown as a rambler, often exceeding 12ft (3.6m), or, in cooler climates, as a good-sized shrub.

Kathleen

HEIGHT *6ft (2m) as a shrub or 10ft (3m) as a climber*
SPREAD *4ft (1.2m) as a shrub or 6ft (2m) as a climber*
FLOWERING *Repeat* TYPE *Hybrid musk*
SCENT *Medium to strong musk* ZONES *6–11*

Although it has the look of a wild rose, this rose is, in fact, a hybrid musk bred by Pemberton and, so, has good repeat flowering. The single flowers start as blush, quickly changing to pure white, and the long stamens emit a delicious fragrance. They are produced in large heads of up to 30 blooms, and if not dead-headed a crop of small red hips follow. In addition to a large shrub, it also makes a superb climber. Almost thornless and very healthy. Slightly smaller than 'Kathleen', but otherwise similarly lovely, is 'Lyda Rose'.

Rosa primula

HEIGHT *6ft (2m)* SPREAD *8ft (2.5m)* FLOWERING *Once*
TYPE *Species rose* SCENT *Light, but the leaves smell strongly*
ZONES *6–9*

This is one of the few roses whose leaves have a distinct smell. On humid evenings, or if crushed, they smell strongly of incense. They are attractive in their own right, with as many as 15 slender leaflets on each stem. *Rosa primula* starts flowering early in the year, the flowers being a pale primrose-yellow. They are followed by round red hips, although these aren't showy. Like the other species roses, it should be allowed to grow without any pruning.

'Kathleen'

Rosa primula

'Boscobel'

Roses for scent

Perfume is an essential aspect of the mystique and character of many roses, and it comes in a surprising variety of aromas—not just the classic old rose, but all kinds of fruity and spicy notes. While countless roses are scented, these outstandingly fragrant varieties are roses to plant beside your favorite seat in the garden, to enjoy as you relax.

Stanwell Perpetual

HEIGHT *5ft (1.5m)* SPREAD *5ft (1.5m)*
FLOWERING *Repeat* TYPE *Spinossisima hybrid*
SCENT *Fragrance strong old rose* ZONES *3–9*

A beautiful rose of unknown origin, it appeared in a cottage garden in 1838 with, fairly obviously, *R. spinosissima* as one parent and perhaps, as it repeat-flowers, Perpetual Damask as the other. Blooms are a soft-pink, old rose in character, and have a strong, delicious, pure old-rose fragrance. Even out of flower it is attractive, with a graceful habit and grayish-green leaves. A substantial, healthy shrub that copes well with poor soil and needs little pruning.

'Stanwell Perpetual'

Boscobel

HEIGHT *3ft (1m)* SPREAD *3ft (1m)* FLOWERING *Repeat*
TYPE *David Austin English rose* SCENT *Strong myrrh*
CULTIVAR *'Auscousin'* ZONES *5–11*

One of the strongest and most distinctive fragrances to be
found in the English roses—essentially myrrh with additional
hints of hawthorn, elderflower, pear, and almond. The
flowers are cup-shaped, filled with many petals varying in
color from pink through to apricot. A healthy and fairly
upright shrub with upward-pointing blooms; perfect for the
mixed border.

Paul's Himalayan Musk

HEIGHT *40ft (12m)* SPREAD *16ft (5m)* FLOWERING *Once*
TYPE *Rambler* SCENT *Strong musk* ZONES *5–8*

Although not quite in the top league for vigor, this rose
certainly is tops for its strong musk fragrance, which wafts
from it for some distance. This comes from the vast numbers
of small, semi-double, soft-pink flowers. Since it is such a big
rose, it should only be grown into a big tree, otherwise it will
be a real challenge to keep under control. It may take a few
years to create a good show, but it is well worth the wait if
you have the space.

Buttercup

HEIGHT *5ft (1.5m)* SPREAD *4ft (1.2m)*
FLOWERING *Repeat* TYPE *David Austin English rose*
SCENT *Strong* CULTIVAR *'Ausband'* ZONES *5–9*

For many years, the fragrances of the roses at David Austin
Roses were identified by Robert Calkin. He was an expert at
describing them, naming each element. The exception was
'Buttercup', for which he could only offer "strong and
delicious." It is sometimes reminiscent of orange blossom
and just occasionally cocoa powder! The flowers are semi-
double, a pure golden-yellow, and held in large, open sprays.
It can get quite tall, so is best toward the back of a mixed
border—but make sure it is still accessible.

'Paul's Himalayan Musk'

'Buttercup'

Cape Diamond

HEIGHT *4ft (1.2m)*
SPREAD *3ft (1m)*
FLOWERING *Repeat*
TYPE *Shrub* SCENT *Strong sweet*
CULTIVAR *'Darpellerin'* ZONES *3–8*

A rose that does not get disease at all, it has a lovely, strong, spicy fragrance. The semi-double flowers are pure pink and large. If not dead-headed, they produce red hips, but flowers should be removed to encourage better repeat flowering. It can be kept as a tall shrub or pruned lightly to make a short climber. Remarkably winter-hardy.

Jacques Cartier

HEIGHT *4ft (1.2m)*
SPREAD *3ft (1m)*
FLOWERING *Repeat* TYPE *Portland*
SCENT *Strong old rose* ZONES *5–11*

Also known as 'Marchesa Boccella', this variety is arguably the best of the Portlands. The fragrance is strong, pure old rose, and the flowers epitomize an old rose, with their mass of petals beautifully arranged around a central eye. The growth is upright, so it's best grown with other plants around it. It will cope well with significant shade. An excellent all-arounder.

Graham Thomas

HEIGHT *4ft (1.2m) or 10ft (3m)*
as climber SPREAD *4ft (1.2m)*
FLOWERING *Repeat*
TYPE *David Austin English rose*
SCENT *Medium to strong tea*
CULTIVAR *'Ausmas'* ZONES *5–9*

Tea fragrance can sometimes be hard to recognize, but in 'Graham Thomas' it is obvious and particularly delicious, with a lovely cool violet character. This rose can be grown as a reasonably tall shrub or, in a warm location, makes an excellent climber. The flowers are cup-shaped and an extraordinarily rich shade of yellow.

Munstead Wood

HEIGHT *4ft (1.2m)*
SPREAD *3ft (1m)*
FLOWERING *Repeat*
TYPE *David Austin English rose*
SCENT *Fruity old rose* CULTIVAR
'Ausbernard' ZONES *5–10*

A richly colored rose with a rich fragrance—a perfect mix of old rose and fruit (specifically blackberry, blueberry, and damson). The blooms are large, full-petaled, and a deep, velvety crimson, a little paler on the undersides of the petals. It will make a real impact in a border, especially when planted next to blue flowers. Responds to a little extra care and attention. Very thorny!

Sophie's Perpetual

HEIGHT *5ft (1.5m)*
SPREAD *4ft (1.2m)*
FLOWERING *Repeat*
TYPE *Hybrid China*
SCENT *Strong* ZONES *7–10*

Robert Calkin described the scent of 'Sophie's Perpetual' as the closest to a real perfume, and it is indeed delicious. The flowers are medium-sized, a soft pink that darkens with age—normal for the Chinas but unusual for most other roses—to a light crimson. It takes some time to build up to a substantial shrub and so is best pruned lightly. A pretty and rather unusual rose.

Savannah

HEIGHT *4ft (1.2m)* SPREAD *3ft (1m)*
FLOWERING *Repeat* TYPE *Hybrid tea*
SCENT *Very strong fruit*
CULTIVAR *'Korvioros'* ZONES *5–10*

The blooms of 'Savannah' are similar to those of the once-flowering old roses, although they repeat-flower well and have a strong, fruity fragrance. Their color is soft salmon-pink, verging on pure pink, and each has around 150 petals! The variety is extremely healthy, with nice compact growth. Winner of three awards at the Biltmore International Rose Trials, including overall best rose. Does well in both hot, humid and hot, dry conditions.

'Ispahan'

'Constance Spry'

Ispahan

HEIGHT *5ft (1.5m)* SPREAD *4ft (1.2m)* FLOWERING *Once*
TYPE *Damask* SCENT *Strong old rose* ZONES *4–10*

One of the very best of the old roses, 'Ispahan' has beautiful
blooms and a strong and delicious old-rose fragrance. The
flowers are pure mid-pink and open to perfectly formed
rosettes. It is the first of the damasks to start flowering
and the last to stop. It also has the advantage of being
semi-evergreen.

Constance Spry

HEIGHT *6ft (2m) or 10ft (3m) as a climber* SPREAD *6ft (2m)*
FLOWERING *Once* TYPE *David Austin English rose*
SCENT *Strong myrrh* CULTIVAR *'Ausfirst'* ZONES *5–9*

'Constance Spry' was David Austin's very first rose,
introduced in 1961. It has large, pure rose-pink flowers with
an extremely strong myrrh fragrance, which until that time
was practically unknown. Can be grown as a large shrub,
although it works much better as a climber, when it will
make a most impressive and beautiful show.

Gertrude Jekyll

HEIGHT *5ft (1.5m) or 10ft (3m) as climber* SPREAD *3ft (1m)*
FLOWERING *Repeat* TYPE *David Austin English rose*
SCENT *Strong old rose* CULTIVAR *'Ausbord'* ZONES *4–9*

Of all roses, 'Gertrude Jekyll' is one of the very best for
fragrance—a strong, classic, and delicious old-rose type.
The blooms are lovely—large and pure pink, the petals
arranged in the form of a rosette. As a medium-sized shrub,
it is lovely mixed in with other plants. It also makes an
excellent climber (p.213).

Hansa

HEIGHT *6ft (2m)* SPREAD *5ft (1.5m)*
FLOWERING *Repeat* TYPE *Rugosa hybrid*
SCENT *Strong old rose* ZONES *3–9*

The rugosa roses are well-known for being particularly tough and winter-hardy, bearing large hips, and having a delicious fragrance. 'Hansa' is excellent on all those counts. The double flowers are a bright magenta-pink and are followed by large red hips. The old-rose fragrance is strong and delicious. A big, thorny rose that is wonderful in a hedge or a mixed border.

'Hansa'

'Lady Emma Hamilton'

'Königin von Dänemark'

Lady Emma Hamilton

HEIGHT *3ft (1m)* SPREAD *3ft (1m)* FLOWERING *Repeat*
TYPE *David Austin English rose* SCENT *Strong fruity*
CULTIVAR *'Ausbrother'* ZONES *5–9*

A delicious fragrance to put a smile on your face! It is
made up of a rich mix of fruits—citrus with strong
hints of pear and grape, and sometimes even guava and
lychee. 'Lady Emma Hamilton' is also notable for the
dark bronzy color of its leaves, especially when young.
The blooms are cup-shaped and a lovely mix of rich
tangerine-orange on the inside of the petals and orange-
yellow on the reverse. It can sometimes require a little
extra care and attention to keep it growing and
flowering well.

Königin von Dänemark

HEIGHT *5ft (1.5m)* SPREAD *3ft (1m)* FLOWERING *Once*
TYPE *Alba* SCENT *Strong old rose* ZONES *4–9*

One of the most beautiful of the old roses, also known
as 'Queen of Denmark'. The pure soft-pink flowers, the
color deepening in the center where the petals are
packed together, are quartered with a central button
eye. They are beautifully set off by gray-green leaves.
The classic old-rose fragrance is particularly delicious.
If pruned each winter, the growth is upright, but
becomes more spreading and arching otherwise.
A tough and reliable rose.

Rambling Rector

HEIGHT *26ft (8m)*   SPREAD *16ft (5m)*
FLOWERING *Once*   TYPE *Rambler*
SCENT *Strong musk*   ZONES *6–9*

This is one of the best known of the ramblers, partly because of its name, but also because it is a very good rose. When in flower, the leaves are barely visible because of the mass of semi-double, white flowers. The combined strength of the fragrance of so many thousands of flowers is impressive and can be detected from some distance away. Many small orange hips follow the flowers. 'Rambling Rector' is extremely vigorous and needs to be sited with care, preferably to grow up a large tree (p.216). The equally large 'Seagull' is similar, if not identical, and they are often mixed up by nurseries.

Autumn Damask

HEIGHT *6ft (2m)*   SPREAD *5ft (1.5m)*
FLOWERING *Repeat*   TYPE *Damask*
SCENT *Strong old rose*   ZONES *4–9*

'Autumn Damask' is also known as 'Quatre Saisons' and as *R. x damascena* var. *bifera* or *semperflorens*. As its names suggest, it repeat flowers—almost unheard of for a rose dating back to around 1660. The flowers are loosely double and a pure rose-pink. Robert Calkin, the rose fragrance expert, said if sunshine had a fragrance it would be like this rose. It is not the tidiest of shrubs, but surrounding it with perennials does help to disguise this weak point.

White Licorice

HEIGHT *4ft (1.2m)*   SPREAD *3ft (1m)*
FLOWERING *Repeat*   TYPE *Floribunda*   SCENT *Strong*
CULTIVAR *'Wekdidusinra'*   ZONES *5–9*

As the name suggests, this rose's fragrance has a strong hint of licorice, although there is a lovely lemony addition in there, too. 'White Licorice' is a floribunda, even though the young flowers are more like a hybrid tea, and, at that stage, a soft lemon-yellow color. As they age, the petals open up to reveal the stamens, and they become white or creamy. A free-flowering variety, good for cutting.

Madame Legras de Saint Germain

HEIGHT *6ft (2m) or 8ft (2.5m) as a climber*
SPREAD *5ft (1.5m)*   FLOWERING *Once*   TYPE *Alba*
SCENT *Strong old rose*   ZONES *5–9*

A rather mystery rose, its parentage is not known and it is not clear to which group it really belongs. It is nevertheless a worthwhile addition to the garden, especially as good roses with white flowers are scarce. The blooms are double, with many petals spiraling around a central eye. It can be grown as a somewhat lax shrub or, better, as a climber. It has the added attribute of being thornless.

'Rambling Rector'

'White Licorice'

'Autumn Damask'

'Madame Legras de St. Germain'

Roses for cutting

Being able to cut roses for the house is one of
the great delights of growing them. Garden
roses may not last as long as florists' flowers, but
they have much more character and fragrance.
With choices ranging from wild roses to
hybrid teas, they will work in just about any
style of arrangement.

'Queen of Sweden'

Queen of Sweden

HEIGHT *4ft (1.2m)* SPREAD *3ft (1m)* FLOWERING *Repeat*
TYPE *English rose* SCENT *Medium myrrh* CULTIVAR *'Austiger'*
ZONES *5–10*

The English roses are generally known for their bushy, sometimes lax growth, which can make beautiful, relaxed flower arrangements, but if you want one with stiffer, straighter stems, 'Queen of Sweden' is the best choice. The petals are arranged tightly in the form of a neat rosette, which starts as a soft peach and gradually changes to pale pink. The fragrance is somewhat variable, but at its best, it is a good myrrh. This is a narrow, upright shrub, and to create a show is best planted in a small group. Also a good choice for a hedge (p.164).

Rosa glauca

HEIGHT *6ft (2m)* SPREAD *5ft (1.5m)* FLOWERING *Once*
TYPE *Species rose* SCENT *Little or none* ZONES *2–9*

While the flowers of *Rosa glauca* are pretty and are certainly effective in arrangements, it is the rose's young growth, with plum-purple to slate-gray leaves, that is most valued by florists. The stems are also an attractive purple with a white bloom. If you want to encourage these young stems, you will need to prune at least part of the rose hard each winter. It also bears an excellent crop of bright-red hips in the fall.

Roald Dahl

HEIGHT *3ft (1m)* SPREAD *3ft (1m)* FLOWERING *Repeat*
TYPE *English rose* SCENT *Medium tea* CULTIVAR *'Ausowlish'*
ZONES *5–10*

A lovely rose for making relaxed arrangements. In contrast to the orange-red buds, the open flowers are pure apricot. They are medium-sized, don't have too many petals, and so aren't too heavy, making them easier to arrange. In a vase, as in the garden, the flowers will blend beautifully with a wide range of other colors, but are especially effective with lilacs and lavenders. 'Roald Dahl' has a lovely tea fragrance and is very healthy.

Rosa glauca

'Roald Dahl'

Chandos Beauty

HEIGHT *4ft (1.2m)* SPREAD *3ft (1m)*
FLOWERING *Repeat* TYPE *Hybrid tea*
SCENT *Strong sweet*
CULTIVAR *'Harmisty'*
ZONES *6–9*

'Chandos Beauty' is an excellent choice for a classic hybrid-tea flower in arrangements. The blooms have the high-pointed center along with a strong and delicious fragrance. The color is a lovely mix of amber-gold and cream, with occasional pink flushes. The plant is strong and robust, with dark, disease-resistant leaves. It works equally well in a formal bed or a mixed border.

Desmond Tutu

HEIGHT *4ft (1.2m)*
SPREAD *3ft (1m)*
FLOWERING *Repeat*
TYPE *Hybrid tea*
SCENT *Light to moderate*
CULTIVAR *'Kortutu'*
ZONES *5–11*

The young flowers of 'Desmond Tutu' have the perfect hybrid-tea form, opening nicely to a full-petaled bloom. When cut, they last well in the house, and a bouquet of these makes a perfect gift. The leaves are a shiny, dark green, and very healthy. The variety is tolerant of a wide range of conditions, including hot and dry, and doesn't mind shade or a coastal garden.

"Consider every stage of a rose: the bud is often a very different color from the open flower, which may change dramatically again as it fades."

Pride of England

HEIGHT *3ft (1m)*
SPREAD *2ft (60cm)*
FLOWERING *Repeat*
TYPE *Hybrid tea* SCENT *Medium*
CULTIVAR *'Harencore'* ZONES *5–10*

A classic, red, hybrid-tea rose. The fragrant flowers are borne on stiff stems and are very large—4in (12cm) across—and a dark red, making them a good choice for more formal arrangements or for giving to a loved one. The bush is vigorous and will quickly replace any stems taken for cutting. It may need some protection from cold winter winds.

Pink Enchantment

HEIGHT *3ft (1m)*
SPREAD *2½ft (75cm)*
FLOWERING *Repeat*
TYPE *Hybrid tea*
SCENT *Medium to strong fruity*
CULTIVAR *'Korsouba'*
ZONES *5–9*

A lovely, healthy rose for both the border and for cutting, which also goes by the name of 'Souvenir de Baden Baden'. It is typical in producing just one to three blooms per stem, and the bud form is the common high-pointed center. The petals have a distinctive scalloped edge. Unlike many hybrid teas, which tend to lose their form once open, 'Pink Enchantment' stays attractive. In bud, it is a soft cream with a slight hint of peachy-pink, which becomes more prevalent once open. It has a delicious fruity fragrance that combines lychee, plum, and elderflower. With its long vase life, it makes a wonderful cutting rose.

Sunny Sky

HEIGHT *4ft (1.2m)* SPREAD *3ft (1m)*
FLOWERING *Repeat* TYPE *Hybrid tea*
SCENT *Light to medium fruity*
CULTIVAR *'Koraruli'* ZONES *5–9*

Whether you prefer a hybrid-tea-type bloom or that of an old rose, 'Sunny Sky' has all the characteristics needed for a good cut flower. The flowers start in the classic hybrid-tea form, but rather than losing their form, these, with their beautifully arranged petals, become old-roselike over time. The color is a lovely honey-yellow that pales with age. Health is important when choosing varieties for cutting, and 'Sunny Sky', a European award-winner, has excellent health. The fragrance, while not strong, is delicious. Stems are robust and upright, making it easy to arrange and a good choice for the border.

'James L. Austin'

James L. Austin

HEIGHT *4ft (1.2m)*   SPREAD *3ft (1m)*
FLOWERING *Repeat*   TYPE *English rose*
SCENT *Light to medium fruity*   CULTIVAR *'Auspike'*
ZONES *5–11*

In form, the flowers of 'James L. Austin' are much like those of the Portland 'Jacques Cartier', with many petals beautifully arranged around a central button eye. The color, however, is several shades darker—a deep pink. The growth is quite bushy. A healthy rose, good in all parts of the garden. With its fruity fragrance, it is lovely in an arrangement.

Silas Marner

HEIGHT *3ft (1m)*   SPREAD *4½ft (1.4m)*
FLOWERING *Repeat*   TYPE *English rose*
SCENT *Medium to strong old rose*
CULTIVAR *'Ausraveloe'*   ZONES *5–10*

With its arching stems, 'Silas Marner' looks lovely in more informal arrangements mixed in with other flowers. Likewise, in the garden, this is a good choice for a mixed border. The medium-sized, cup-shaped flowers are soft pink, paler toward the outside and on the undersides of the petals. The medium-strong old-rose fragrance has hints of fruity lemon, green banana, and apricot. A very healthy rose.

'Silas Marner'

157

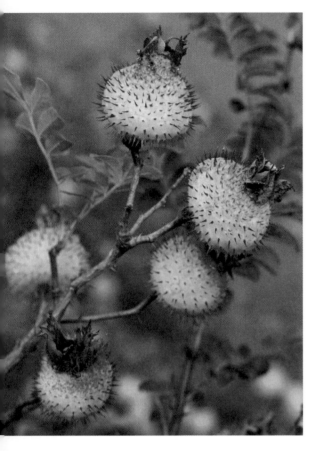

Rosa roxburghii

Roses for
hips, leaves
& thorns

Roses aren't just about flowers. Some have fragrant leaves, while others are prized for their hips, which come in all shapes, sizes, and colors and often last well into the winter. One variety is even grown for its eye-catching thorns, which look wonderful when backlit.

"Rose hips come in a wide variety of shapes, sizes, and colors and are of huge value to wildlife."

'Tottering-by-Gently'

Rosa roxburghii

HEIGHT *6ft (2m)* SPREAD *6ft (2m)* FLOWERING *Single*
TYPE *Wild rose* SCENT *Light or none* ZONES *6–9*

A distinctive rose not only for its hips, but also for its flowers.
The common name, chestnut rose, comes from the similarity
of the hip to the fruit of the horse chestnut, with its many
soft spines. The hips are large, flattened spheres that don't
turn orange or red like those of most roses, but a soft yellow.
The large, five-petaled flowers are soft pink with a white
center. It makes a big shrub and so needs plenty of space. It is
also unusual for having peeling bark and many leaflets to
each leaf. Another form of roxburghii has double-flowers,
but doesn't set hips.

Tottering-by-Gently

HEIGHT *4ft (1.2m)* SPREAD *4ft (1.2m)* FLOWERING *Repeat*
TYPE *David Austin English rose* SCENT *Light to medium musk*
CULTIVAR *'Auscartoon'* ZONES *5–10*

The majority of roses that set a good crop of hips are
large, often 6ft (2m) or more, and tricky to fit into smaller
gardens. 'Tottering-by-Gently', on the other hand, is
medium-sized and its single yellow flowers look good in a
mixed border. If not dead-headed, it produces a heavy crop
of medium-sized orange hips in early fall that last through
the winter. A very good, tough, and reliable rose.

Rosa sericea subsp. *omeiensis* f. *pteracantha*

HEIGHT *8ft (2.5m)* SPREAD *6ft (2m)* FLOWERING *Once*
TYPE *Species rose* SCENT *Little or none* ZONES *6–9*

When seen with the sun shining through them, the large,
broad, blood-red thorns of this rose (also known as
R. omeiensis 'Pteracantha') put on a brilliant show. They are
only red in the first year, so to ensure a good supply of young
stems, the rose should be pruned quite heavily each year. The
flowers, which are only produced on older stems, are small,
white, and have just four petals. The hips are small and bright
red, but drop off as soon as they are ripe.

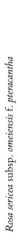

Rosa sericea subsp. omeiensis f. pteracantha

'William Lobb'

Rosa rubiginosa

HEIGHT *8ft (2.5m); often more* SPREAD *8ft (2.5m);*
often more FLOWERING *Once* TYPE *Species rose*
SCENT *Light to medium* ZONES *5–9*

The sweet briar (also known as *R. eglantaria*, or
eglantine) is native to the British Isles and much of
Europe. It is similar to the dog rose, although the
flowers are a little darker and the stems much more
thorny (indeed, ferociously so). The flowers are
followed by shiny, rich-red oval hips that last into the
winter. After rain, or if crushed lightly, the young
leaves smell just like green apples. For the best
fragrance, you'll need to keep cutting the stems back,
although this will mean no flowers or hips unless you
leave a few to keep growing. Thrives in alkaline soils.

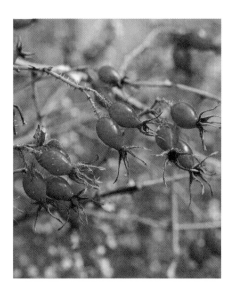

Rosa rubiginosa

William Lobb

HEIGHT *8ft (2.5m)* SPREAD *5ft (1.5m)* FLOWERING *Once*
TYPE *Moss rose* SCENT *Strong* ZONES *5–9*

'William Lobb' is one of the most disease-resistant of the moss roses. It has large, dark-crimson flowers that turn a shade of lavender as they age. These are strongly fragrant, and the "moss" also has a delicious, resinous smell. Leave 'William Lobb' unpruned to form a climber—it will grow 10–13ft (3–4m) up into a tree, for instance—or keep it pruned as a shrub, 5–6ft (1.5–2m) tall.

Easy on the Eyes

HEIGHT *3ft (1m)* SPREAD *3ft (1m)* FLOWERING *Repeat*
TYPE *Shrub* SCENT *Light* CULTIVAR *'Wekswechefy'*
ZONES *5–9*

Rosa persica was previously called *Hulthemia persica* and, hence, not considered a rose at all. The leaves are not divided, and the strong yellow flowers have a distinctive red eye. Breeders tried to introduce this character into modern, repeat-flowering roses. Jack Harkness was the first, with 'Tigris' (in 1975) and 'Euphrates' (in 1980). Both, sadly, are susceptible to blackspot, as *R. persica* is native to the dry climates of Iran, Afghanistan, and central Asia, where blackspot is never seen. A recent resurgence in interest has resulted in several good, repeat-flowering varieties with dark centers. 'Easy on the Eyes' is one of the best, with semi-double pink flowers and a dark purple heart. Flowers freely and stays healthy.

Rosa rugosa 'Alba'

HEIGHT *4ft (1.2m)* SPREAD *4ft (1.2m)* FLOWERING *Repeat*
TYPE *Species rose* SCENT *Strong old rose* ZONES *2–9*

The hips of this rose and the original pink *Rosa rugosa* are bright-red, shiny, and the size of cherry tomatoes. They follow wide-open, single, white flowers that are produced from early summer to late fall, a rarity in wild roses. *Rosa rugosa* grows on the coasts of northern Japan, North Korea, Siberia, and northeastern China. In gardens, its thorny stems can create an impenetrable hedge. Incredibly tough and winter-hardy, it thrives in poor soil where little else will grow. Equally effective in a mixed border. Disease-resistant.

'Easy on the Eyes'

Rosa rugosa 'Alba'

'The Generous Gardener'

Rosa spinosissima

The Generous Gardener

HEIGHT *6ft (2m) or 13ft (4m) as a climber*
SPREAD *10ft (3m)* FLOWERING *Repeat*
TYPE *David Austin climbing English rose*
SCENT *Strong old rose, musk, and myrrh*
CULTIVAR *'Ausdrawn'* ZONES *5–10*

A wonderful climber that, if not dead-headed, will bear a superb crop of large orange-red hips that last right through the winter. Allowing the hips to grow may reduce the number of flowers produced later in the season, but it is a sacrifice worth making. The flowers are large, loosely double, and blush pink, paling with age. They open to look charmingly like waterlilies and have a most delicious fragrance. 'The Generous Gardener' can be grown as a large arching shrub, but is better trained as a climber. The young leaves are a bright bronze color and stay very healthy.

Rosa spinosissima

HEIGHT *3ft (1m) (often less)* SPREAD *Indefinite—spreads by suckers* FLOWERING *Once* TYPE *Species rose*
SCENT *Medium to strong* ZONES *3–9*

Known as the Scotch or burnet rose, and also as *R. pimpinellifolia*, this and some of its hybrids are the only roses to bear black hips. Its leaves have many small, dark leaflets. The flowers are single and creamy white and have a delicious fragrance. An incredibly tough rose, it is very low-growing in the wild, where it even grows on sand dunes, but it gets taller in better soils.

Geranium

HEIGHT *8ft (2.5m)* SPREAD *8ft (2.5m)* FLOWERING *Once*
TYPE *Species rose* SCENT *Light* ZONES *3–8*

Also known as *Rosa moyesii* 'Geranium', this may well be the best-known rose for hips. They don't last all that long, but they are striking—pendulous, flagon-shaped, and bright vermillion-red. The single flowers are the same shade of red, enhanced by yellow stamens. It is a big rose, so needs to be planted where there is room for it to reach its full potential.

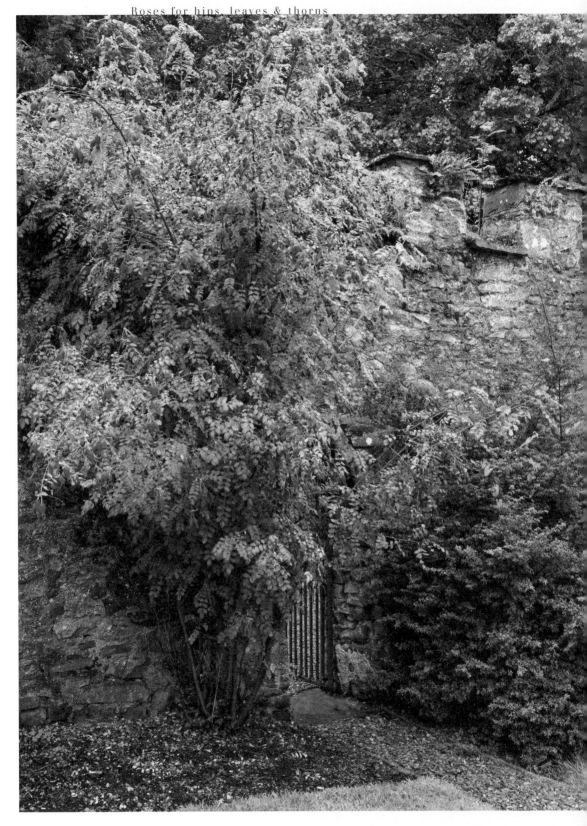

'Geranium'

Roses for hedges

Roses can be grown in every style and height of hedge, from short and formal to tall and impenetrable. Rose hedges are colorful and fragrant, and they can be a valuable source of food and shelter for a wide variety of wildlife.

Kosmos

HEIGHT *3ft (100cm)* SPREAD *2ft (60cm)*
FLOWERING *Repeat* TYPE *Floribunda* SCENT *Light*
CULTIVAR *'Korpriggos'* ZONES *6–9*

The neat, upright growth and first-class resistance to disease make this a perfect choice for a formal hedge inside the garden. It is described as a floribunda, which suggests a rather loose flower, but the flowers are, in fact, full of nicely arranged petals. A peachy color at first, it pales to cream with age. Recipient of a European award for good health.

Queen of Sweden

HEIGHT *4ft (1.2m)* SPREAD *3ft (1m)* FLOWERING *Repeat*
TYPE *David Austin English rose* SCENT *Medium myrrh*
CULTIVAR *'Austiger'* ZONES *5–9*

With its upright, rather narrow growth, 'Queen of Sweden' is perfect for a neat, internal boundary in a garden. The flowers are neat, too—upward-facing, medium-sized rosettes that start a soft apricot before slowly changing to soft pink as they age. The fragrance, though not strong, is a soft and particularly delicious myrrh. 'Queen of Sweden' repeat-flowers well and is very healthy.

'Kosmos'

'Queen of Sweden'

Double Knock Out

HEIGHT *4ft (1.2m)*
SPREAD *4ft (1.2m)*
FLOWERING *Repeat*   TYPE *Shrub*
SCENT *Light*   CULTIVAR *'Radtko'*
ZONES *5–11*

The 'Knock Out' series revolutionized roses when the first one was introduced in 2000. Since then, a number of forms have been introduced; many, if not all, excellent as hedges. As the name suggests, 'Double Knock Out' has more petals (about 20) than the original, but the same cherry-red color. With its ability to flower freely and its excellent health, it makes a good choice for a hedge.

Home Run

HEIGHT *4ft (1.2m)* SPREAD *3ft (1m)*
FLOWERING *Repeat*   TYPE *Shrub*
SCENT *None*   CULTIVAR *'Wekcisbako'*
ZONES *5–9*

When 'Knock Out' was first introduced in 2000, it wasn't long before breeders tried to breed from it. This is one of the first efforts, bred by Tom Carruth and introduced in 2006. It is similar, but healthier, especially for powdery mildew. The flowers have just five petals, as opposed to a few more with 'Knock Out', which means the stamens are prominent and add to its beauty. The color is a true red that fades little, if at all. Incredibly free-flowering and repeats well. A perfect hedging rose.

Topaz Jewel

HEIGHT *4ft (1.2m)* SPREAD *3ft (1m)*
FLOWERING *Repeat*   TYPE *Rugosa*
SCENT *Medium*   ZONES *4–8*

Rosa rugosa and its forms and hybrids make perfect hedging roses, as they are tough, repeat-flowering, fragrant, and often devoid of disease. While 'Topaz Jewel' is not 100 percent healthy, it is still very good. With its thorny stems, it makes an effective barrier. The semi-double, fragrant flowers are yolk yellow at first, fading to lemon, cream, and white. Also known as 'Yellow Dagmar Hastrup', it is a tough and winter-hardy variety.

Kew Gardens

HEIGHT *4ft (1.2m)*
SPREAD *4ft (1.2m)*
FLOWERING *Repeat* TYPE *David Eustin English rose* SCENT *Little or none* CULTIVAR *'Ausfence'*
ZONES *5–11*

'Kew Gardens' makes a first-class hedging rose. It produces its single white flowers incredibly freely from the ground up and it repeats extremely well. It has the great advantage of being completely thornless—useful when mowing close to it. It is also an effective rose in mixed borders. A very healthy variety.

Thomas à Becket

HEIGHT *5ft (1.5m)*
SPREAD *4ft (1.2m)*
FLOWERING *Repeat* TYPE *David Austin English rose* SCENT *Medium old rose* CULTIVAR *'Auswinston'*
ZONES *5–9*

Good red roses suitable for hedges are difficult to find, with 'Thomas à Becket' being a rare exception. It is closely related to wild roses, giving it a distinctive appearance. Its growth is quite upright but very bushy, and eventually slightly arching. The bright crimson flowers start as shallow cups, before opening to informal rosettes, the outer petals reflexing back. It makes a showy and substantial hedge.

Mortimer Sackler

HEIGHT *6ft (2m)* SPREAD *4ft (1.2m)*
FLOWERING *Repeat*
TYPE *David Austin English rose*
SCENT *Light-to-medium fruity old rose* CULTIVAR *'Ausorts'*
ZONES *5–11*

'Mortimer Sackler' is always easy to recognize, with its medium-sized flowers and distinctive leaves and stems. The buds are rose pink, opening to soft-pink, loosely double flowers that pale toward the outside and with age. They are beautifully set off by the dark leaves and dark, almost thornless stems. It can be grown as a short climber and equally easily kept as a tall shrub—it makes a beautiful, airy, informal hedge, as it has so few thorns. Lovely for back of the border, too.

Olivia Rose Austin

HEIGHT *4ft (1.2m)* SPREAD *3ft (1m)* FLOWERING *Repeat*
TYPE *David Austin English rose* SCENT *Light to medium fruity*
CULTIVAR *'Ausmixture'* ZONES *5–11*

Any rose chosen for a hedge, or any other kind of mass
planting, needs to be especially healthy, and 'Olivia Rose
Austin' is ideal. It also has a long flowering season,
starting about two to three weeks before most others and
then repeating very quickly. The soft-pink flowers are
big, with many petals beautifully arranged in a rosette.

Harlow Carr

HEIGHT *3ft (1m)* SPREAD *3ft (1m)*
FLOWERING *Repeat* TYPE *David Austin English rose*
SCENT *Medium to strong old rose* CULTIVAR *'Aushouse'*
ZONES *5–11*

'Harlow Carr' is extremely thorny, with stems that arch
over and intermingle to make an excellent, impenetrable
hedge. The flowers are medium-sized, rose-pink, and
deliciously fragrant. A very healthy rose that could be
planted in a number of places in the garden, both
formal and informal.

'Harlow Carr'

'Olivia Rose Austin'

Roses for warm, sunny walls

Although all roses need at least a few
hours of sun a day, the plants featured here are
real sun-worshippers. They'll appreciate good soil
and regular watering, and reward you with an
abundance of flowers and plenty of perfume.

'Aloha'

Aloha

HEIGHT *10ft (3m)* SPREAD *6ft (2m)* FLOWERING *Repeat*
TYPE *Climber* SCENT *Strong fruity* ZONES *5–10*

'Aloha' was bred by Eugene Boerner and introduced in 1949.
He bred a wide range of plants, but is best known for his
floribundas. This, however, is a climber, and one of his best
varieties. In his quest for extra strength, good repeat-flowering,
and better disease resistance, David Austin used it as the basis
for his 'Leander' roses. 'Aloha' is quite healthy and can be
grown as either a tall shrub or a short climber. The large, fully
double flowers give the impression of being simply a rich pink,
but closer examination shows there is a hint of apricot, too. It
has a glorious fruity fragrance and repeat-flowers well.

Climbing Étoile de Hollande

HEIGHT *13ft (4m)* SPREAD *8ft (2.5m)* FLOWERING *Repeat*
TYPE *Hybrid tea* SCENT *Strong old rose* ZONES *6–10*

'Étoile de Hollande' is one of the very best roses for scent. It is
powerful and delicious—a rich, sweet, old-rose fragrance.
The rich, velvety crimson flowers are a little formless when
fully out, but a classic hybrid-tea shape at first. This is a
vigorous climber and needs plenty of space, although the long
stems are easy to fan out. It sets a good crop of large red hips
if not dead-headed. It is a little susceptible to black spot, but
with some extra care and attention it is a wonderful rose to
have in the garden. A versatile rose, it is also suitable for semi-
shady walls (p.192), but avoid sites that get very strong sun.

The Generous Gardener

HEIGHT *13ft (4m)* SPREAD *10ft (3m)* FLOWERING *Repeat*
TYPE *David Austin English rose* SCENT *Strong old rose, tea, myrrh*
CULTIVAR *'Ausdrawn'* ZONES *5–11*

'The Generous Gardener' was initially introduced as a large
shrub, but it soon became evident that it is more successful as
a climber. It is perhaps best trained against a wall, where its
long, stiff stems can be fanned out, but it is also excellent on
an arbor or pergola, where its wonderful fragrance can be
appreciated. The flowers are large and a pure, soft pink, with
a delicious mix of old rose, myrrh, and tea fragrances. If not
dead-headed, it will set a good crop of large orange-red hips.

'Climbing Étoile de Hollande'

'The Generous Gardener'

Ghislaine de Féligonde

HEIGHT *10ft (3m)* SPREAD *6ft (2m)* FLOWERING *Repeat*
TYPE *Rambler* SCENT *Medium musky* ZONES *5–10*

A rose introduced more than 100 years ago, whose
qualities and garden worthiness have only recently
been recognized. It can be grown as a large arching
shrub, but its almost thornless stems and medium vigor
make it ideal for a fence. As long as it is watered well,
the heat from a sunny wall will encourage more flowers.
These are small, double, and vary greatly in color
between soft apricot and pink. A tough, reliable rose.

Polka

HEIGHT *12ft (3.6m)* SPREAD *8ft (2.5m)*
FLOWERING *Repeat* TYPE *Climber* SCENT *Light to
medium fruit* CULTIVAR *'Meltosier'* ZONES *5–9*

A versatile rose that can be grown as a shrub or climber,
depending on climate and pruning. The flowers are
a rich apricot color that fades with age, producing a
charming range of colors over the whole plant. Healthy
and easy to grow.

'Polka'

'Ghislaine de Féligonde'

Eustacia Vye

HEIGHT *6ft (2m)*
SPREAD *4ft (1.2m)*
FLOWERING *Repeat*
TYPE *David Austin English rose*
SCENT *Strong fruity*
CULTIVAR *'Ausegdon'* ZONES *5–11*

Eustacia Vye is normally sold as
a shrub (p.109), but it makes a
superb short climber, perfect for
a fence or warm wall. It is an
excellent variety, with beautiful
blooms that have a strong,
deliciously fruity fragrance. The
flowers start as deep cups,
gradually opening to reveal many
petals that have a slightly ruffled
look to them. A soft, glowing,
apricot-pink that is darker at first
and pales with age.

Golden Gate

HEIGHT *10ft (3m)* SPREAD *6ft (2m)*
FLOWERING *Repeat* TYPE *Climber*
SCENT *Medium sweet fruity*
CULTIVAR *'Korgolgat'* ZONES *5–10*

An extremely healthy variety that
will stand out in every situation in the
garden. The flowers are large, up to
4in (10cm) across, and a bright golden
yellow. They have a particularly
delicious fruity fragrance—citrus
with a strong element of tropical
flowers. 'Golden Gate' is especially
good for walls and fences, even
if they're partly shady. The growth
is not too stiff and can be trained
over an arch.

Madame Plantier

HEIGHT *10ft (3m)*
SPREAD *8ft (2.5m)*
FLOWERING *Once* TYPE *Alba*
SCENT *Strong sweet old rose*
ZONES *4–11*

A beautiful rose that, sadly, is not often seen, probably just because it doesn't repeat-flower. The small buds are soft pink, but open to perfectly white, medium-sized, full-petaled flowers, with the petals perfectly arranged around a little green eye. The fragrance is delicious and strong. With its slim, thornless, arching stems, it can be grown as a rounded shrub, but is perhaps better trained up a wall, fence, or obelisk or planted to scramble into a small tree. It's a noisette/alba cross that combines the hardiness of an alba with a noisette's ability to grow in hot climates.

Climbing Mrs Herbert Stevens

HEIGHT *16ft (5m)*
SPREAD *10ft (3m)*
FLOWERING *Repeat* TYPE *Hybrid tea* SCENT *Strong tea* ZONES *7–9*

First introduced as a climber back in 1922, the excellence of this variety is proven by its age, given how few roses from that time are still grown today. In fact, it was initially bred as a bush rose in 1910; a sport from that produced this climbing form. Both have the most beautiful blooms, with the classic high-point center of the hybrid teas, although more refined than many more modern varieties. The large flowers are pure white, except for a slight yellow tint at the center. They hang down, which is a disadvantage on a bush, but a bonus on a climber. The fragrance is particularly strong and delicious. This is a vigorous climber, and the stems are quite stiff, too—so it needs plenty of space.

Fourth of July

HEIGHT *10ft (3m)*
SPREAD *6ft (2m)*
FLOWERING *Repeat*
TYPE *Climber* SCENT *Medium fruit*
CULTIVAR *'Wekroalt'* ZONES *5–10*

This climber stands out from the rest. The small-to-medium flowers are produced almost continuously in a combination of red and white, the proportion differing greatly from flower to flower. It performs well in many climates and varies considerably in the height it can reach—in cooler regions, it makes a tall shrub; in warmer ones, it is a substantial climber, growing up to 15ft (4.5m).

'Monsieur Tillier'

Roses for
hot, humid
climates

This can be a challenging climate for many
roses, but not all. The varieties showcased
here will all flower and grow beautifully,
even in humid regions where temperatures
can top 90°F (32°C).

'Altissimo'

Monsieur Tillier

HEIGHT *6ft (2m)* SPREAD *3ft (1m)* FLOWERING *Continuous*
TYPE *Tea* SCENT *Strong tea* ZONES *7–11*

The flowers of 'Monsieur Tillier' are classic tea-shaped,
with lots of quill-shaped petals in the middle. It is also
classically tea in that it never stops flowering in hot climates.
The color is a wonderful mix of red, pink, and apricot, with
touches of yellow and coppery pink, and the fragrance
resembles a fruity, sweet tea. A vigorous shrub, especially
in warmer climates.

Altissimo

HEIGHT *10ft (3m)* SPREAD *6ft (2m)* FLOWERING *Repeat*
TYPE *Climber* SCENT *Light clove* ZONES *6–10*

This is a rose that does well in just about any climate. While
the color might be a little more intense in cool regions, it is
still excellent in warm ones. Red roses often burn in hot sun,
but not 'Altissimo'. The petals are completely red right to the
center, setting off the stamens particularly well. If kept
pruned, it can be grown as a large shrub, but is better trained
as a climber. It also repeat-flowers well.

Sally Holmes

HEIGHT *10ft (3m)* SPREAD *6ft (2m)* FLOWERING *Repeat*
TYPE *Climber* SCENT *Light* ZONES *5–10*

'Sally Holmes' in cooler climates is a large shrub, but in
warmer ones, it is an excellent climber. The flowers are large
and single, with the odd extra petal. On the main stems,
they are produced in large heads with many flowers,
sometimes too many, making them look rather crowded.
The side shoots, however, have fewer flowers, and so look
better. The flowers last a long time, both on the plant and
when cut. It is almost thornless.

'Sally Holmes'

Rosa x *odorata* 'Mutabilis'

HEIGHT *6ft (2m)* SPREAD *8ft (2.5m)* FLOWERING *Continuous*
TYPE *China* SCENT *Light* ZONES *7–10*

'Mutabilis' is a mystery rose. Aside from a few varieties
that it parented, there is nothing quite like it. It was first
spotted in 1894 in a garden on Lake Maggiore and
introduced commercially in 1933; nowadays, you may
also find it called 'Butterfly Rose' or 'Tipo Ideale'. The
flowers are truly single, start a soft yellow and, in typical
China fashion, turn pink and eventually a pale or dark
crimson as they age. It prefers a hot or at least warm
climate, be it dry or humid, where it will continuously
flower, but can still look lovely even in more temperate
climates. Growth is graceful and gently arching, but it
can be trained as a climber. Requires little to no pruning.

Ducher

HEIGHT *4ft (1.2m)* SPREAD *3ft (1m)* FLOWERING *Repeat*
TYPE *China/tea* SCENT *Strong fruity* ZONES *7–11*

Generally regarded as the only white China rose,
'Ducher' flowers continuously in warm climates. The
buds are rounded, with an occasional hint of pink and,
when open, are pure white, or nearly so, the swirling
petals filling the flower. It has a delicious, fruity
fragrance. Like most Chinas, the ultimate size depends
very much on the climate where it is planted.

'Ducher'

Rosa x *odorata* 'Mutabilis'

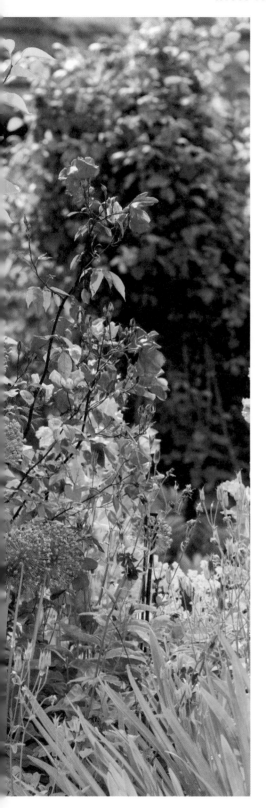

'Général Schablikine'

Général Schablikine

HEIGHT *4ft (1.2m)* SPREAD *4ft (1.2m)*
FLOWERING *Continuous* TYPE *Tea*
SCENT *Medium tea* ZONES *7–11*

One of the best of the teas, it is tough and extremely free-flowering and, in fact, was grown in great quantities in Italy for the winter cut-flower trade, when the flowers are particularly fine. While it is much better in warmer climates, it can be grown in cooler areas in a greenhouse or against a warm wall. The flowers are a beautiful mix of colors, varying according to temperature and age, but are usually a warm rose-pink with a deeper reverse. In the center, the petals are delightfully quilled, with a fawn-yellow undertone that creates a coppery-salmon coloring. The fragrance is fresh, sweet, and floral. It can be grown as a tall shrub or short climber, depending on the climate.

Lamarque

HEIGHT *15ft (4.5m)* SPREAD *10ft (3m)*
FLOWERING *Some repeating* TYPE *Climber tea-noisette*
SCENT *Strong lemon* ZONES *8–11*

This is definitely a rose for warm climates. The flowers are large—the soft lemon-yellow petals that fade to white perfectly arranged in a rosette. It is vigorous, with nearly thornless stems, and benefits from a sheltered spot. A generous crop of flowers early in the season is followed by a good number of sporadic flowers later on. The delicious fragrance wafts on the air.

Crépuscule

HEIGHT *10ft (3m)* SPREAD *5ft (1.5m)* FLOWERING *Repeat*
TYPE *Noisette climber* SCENT *Strong tea* ZONES *7–11*

At the Flemington Race Course in Melbourne, Australia, there is a long fence covered in 'Crépuscule', which, when in flower, creates a superb spectacle. The flowers are a lovely mix of colors, a deep-rich butterscotch and apricot-yellow that fades with age. The leaves, crimson at first, are dark and shiny, setting off the flowers nicely. Excellent repeat-flowering. A fantastic rose in warm climates.

Mrs B. R. Cant

HEIGHT *7ft (2.2m)* SPREAD *6ft (2m)*
FLOWERING *Continuous* TYPE *Tea*
SCENT *Strong fruity* ZONES *7–11*

This is a vigorous shrub that can quickly achieve a height of 6ft (2m). A climbing form is sometimes listed, but is probably dependent on where it is grown and how it is pruned. Buds are pointed, opening to large, very double, cupped blooms of soft pink, darker in the center and in hot weather. The fragrance is strong and delicious—sweet, musky, fruity (passion fruit and peach), with earthy, peppery undertones. In the right climate, it flowers more or less continuously throughout the year. Flower stems are long. Long-lasting when cut.

Cramoisi Supérieur

HEIGHT *6ft (2m)* SPREAD *4ft (1.2m)*
FLOWERING *Continuous* TYPE *China*
SCENT *Light* ZONES *7–11*

A rose with many names, including 'Agrippina', 'Old Bermuda Red Rose', and 'L'Eblouissante'—perhaps a reflection of what a great survivor it is when left untended in adverse conditions. Even in thickets, the bright, dark-crimson flowers are easy to spot. Closer examination of the flower shows that the petal tips are somewhat paler, as are the backs of the petals. In warmer climates, it flowers more or less continuously. It is rare, in fact, not to see it in flower. It can reach a height of 6ft (2m) or more, and there is a climbing form that can grow to double that height.

'Lamarque'

'Mrs B. R. Cant'

'Crépuscule'

'Cramoisi Supérieur'

'Jubilee Celebration'

Roses for
hot, dry
climates

A hot, dry climate can make roses flower
more sparingly and grow wildly. Fortunately,
these varieties will do neither, and will be
a delightful feature in any garden that
experiences this type of climate.

Lemon Fizz

HEIGHT *3ft (1m)*   SPREAD *3ft (1m)*
FLOWERING *Repeat*   TYPE *Modern shrub*
SCENT *Light*   CULTIVAR *'Korfizzlem'*
ZONES *5–11*

A very useful rose that, with its compact
growth, is excellent for brightening up corners
of the garden, patio, or balcony. The unfading,
bright-yellow flowers are produced continuously
and with the stamens fully exposed are much
loved by bees. Extremely healthy and suitable
for planting in both the ground and in pots.

'Lemon Fizz'

Jubilee Celebration

HEIGHT *4ft (1.2m)* SPREAD *4ft (1.2m)* FLOWERING *Repeat*
TYPE *David Austin English rose* SCENT *Strong fruity*
CULTIVAR *'Aushunter'* ZONES *5–11*

An impressive rose with strongly colored, good-sized blooms
that look particularly lovely planted alongside other plants,
especially those with blue-, purple-, or lilac-colored flowers.
With around 90 petals, the flowers are very full, which helps
to produce a strong, fruity (sometimes pure lemon-zest)
fragrance. The color is a rich salmon-pink tinted gold on the
undersides of the petals. A strong and healthy variety.

Kazanlik

HEIGHT *6ft (2m)* SPREAD *5ft (1.5m)* FLOWERING *Single*
TYPE *Damask* SCENT *Strong old rose* ZONES *4–9*

'Kazanlik' is one of the names given to the rose grown in great
quantities in Bulgaria for the production of attar of roses;
others include 'Trigintipetala' and 'Professeur Émile Perrot'.
Being a damask, its growth is arching, so be sure to give it
plenty of space. The flowers are an absolutely pure pink, and in
hot climates, the fragrance is superb. Unfortunately, many
thousands of flowers have to be collected at dawn to produce
tiny quantities of the oil, but the rose is excellent for potpourri.

Elina

HEIGHT *4ft (1.2m)* SPREAD *3ft (1m)* FLOWERING *Repeat*
TYPE *Hybrid tea* SCENT *Light* CULTIVAR *'Dicjana'*
ZONES *6–10*

Introduced in 1983, 'Elina' remains a firm favorite with both
exhibitors and gardeners, doing well in a wide range of
climates. It is an extremely tough, healthy, and vigorous
rose, able to grow to 10ft (3m) or more given the chance. The
creamy-yellow flowers are large and have the perfect high-
centered, hybrid-tea form.

'Kazanlik'

'Elina'

'Iceberg'

Iceberg

HEIGHT *5ft (1.5m)* SPREAD *3ft (1m)* FLOWERING *Repeat*
TYPE *Floribunda* SCENT *Light* CULTIVAR *'Korbin'*
ZONES *5–11*

This well-known rose also goes by 'Fée des Neiges' and
'Schneewittchen'. At its best in hot, dry climates, where
it can flower year-round. Pure-white, semi-double
flowers are produced on open clusters, each bloom long-
lasting and dropping petals cleanly. Impressive as a bush
or as standard in Mediterranean-type climates. It looks
hybrid-musklike and its parentage confirms that. Stems
have few thorns. Early on, it sported to a climbing form;
later, to 'Brilliant Pink Iceberg' and 'Burgundy Ice'.

Belle Portugaise

HEIGHT *18ft (6m)* SPREAD *10ft (3m)*
FLOWERING *Single* TYPE *Climber hybrid gigantea*
SCENT *Strong tea* ZONES *8–11*

This most magnificent rose will, in the right climate,
grow way up into trees. The semi-double flowers are
huge, up to 6in (15cm) across, and a beautiful, translucent
pale-pink. They look particularly lovely when growing
through dark conifers. The fragrance is variable, but
usually a strong, delicious tea. One of the parents—*R.
gigantean*—has the largest flowers of the climbing species
and is an original parent of many modern roses.

'Belle Portugaise'

'Livin' Easy'

'Fortune's Double Yellow'

Livin' Easy

HEIGHT *4ft (1.2m)* SPREAD *3ft (1m)* FLOWERING *Repeat*
TYPE *Floribunda* SCENT *Medium fruity* CULTIVAR *'Harwelcome'*
ZONES *5–10*

'Livin' Easy' is happy to grow in a wide range of climates, from its native England to California. The flowers are produced freely, especially in warm climates and with a plentiful supply of water. They are a showy apricot-orange, with the stamens appearing in the later stages. A good choice for formal rose gardens, although, with the right partners, lovely in a mixed border, too.

Fortune's Double Yellow

HEIGHT *12ft (3.6m)* SPREAD *10ft (3m)* FLOWERING *Single*
TYPE *China* SCENT *Light tea* ZONES *8–11*

Also known as 'Fortune's Yellow', 'Beauty of Glazenwood', and 'Gold of Ophir', this rose makes an unforgettable sight when seen in Mediterranean-type climates and left to grow as a very large, arching shrub. It is the massed effect of so many bright coppery-yellow petals that makes it so wonderful, since the individual blooms are not all that shapely. Magnificent as a free-standing shrub or grown up into a tree, where the many sharp thorns will help it hang on effectively.

Bonica

HEIGHT *4ft (1.2m)* SPREAD *4ft (1.2m)*
FLOWERING *Repeat* TYPE *Modern shrub* SCENT *Light*
CULTIVAR *'Meidomonac'* ZONES *4–9*

A deservedly widely grown, popular rose, also known as 'Bonica 82'. With its compact growth and smallish, bright-pink flowers set against shiny green leaves, it oozes health and sturdiness. The first flowering is a little later than most roses, but it stays in flower for many weeks. Later in the season, if the plant is dead-headed, a second, smaller crop is borne. In that case, a wonderful crop of long-lasting hips is produced.

'Bonica'

'Maman Cochet'

Maman Cochet

HEIGHT *5ft (1.5m)* SPREAD *3ft (1m)* FLOWERING *Repeat*
TYPE *Tea* SCENT *Strong tea* ZONES *7–11*

Once a best-loved rose, this is a first-class choice for a
hot, dry climate. It combines beauty, fragrance, and
continuous flowering with the ability to thrive on
neglect. The large flowers have the classic high-pointed
center of the teas, but, unlike hybrid teas, with just 30
to 40 petals and no definite form, 'Maman Cochet' has
more than 100 petals and the open flower shows off
their quartered arrangement. Color depends on the
flower's age and the weather, but starts cream-colored
infused with raspberry pink, turning to mauve pink.
The strength of fragrance is variable, but delicious—tea
with violet undertones. An excellent cut flower.

Roses for semi-shady walls

North-facing walls and those in partial shade are always a bit of a challenge for climbing plants, but there are quite a few roses that will do well on them, as long as they get at least four hours of direct sun. The shade will help to prevent the blooms from scorching and make them last longer.

'Perennial Blue'

Perennial Blue

HEIGHT *10ft (3m)*   SPREAD *6ft (2m)*
FLOWERING *Repeat*   TYPE *Rambler*   SCENT *Light*
CULTIVAR *'Mehblue'*   ZONES *6–9*

This is a repeat-flowering version of the old rambler 'Veilchenblau', which is delightful, but vigorous, and does not repeat-flower. The blooms of 'Perennial Blue' are similar in size, about 1½in (4cm) across. Semi-double, they start a rich wine-purple, fading to deep lilac. It is vigorous enough to cover a wall or fence without overwhelming it or being hard to manage. A tough rose that copes well with poorer conditions.

Madame Alfred Carrière

HEIGHT *16ft (5m)*   SPREAD *10ft (3m)*
FLOWERING *Repeat*   TYPE *Noisette climber*
SCENT *Strong fruit*   ZONES *6–10*

'Madame Alfred' is popular around the world, since it's tolerant of a wide range of climates as well as positions in the garden. It's a vigorous variety that needs lots of space. The flower buds are pale pink, turning white as soon as they open. They are not particularly shapely but are produced in large quantities and have a deliciously sweet, often strongly grapefruit fragrance. Noisettes are usually a little on the tender side and require sun, but this one is hardy and grows and flowers well in a certain amount of shade. It is best trained against a wall, which is made easier by the fact that it is nearly thornless, although this makes it less suitable for growing into a tree.

'Madame Alfred Carrière'

'City of York'

'Leverkusen'

City of York

HEIGHT *16ft (5m)* SPREAD *10ft (3m)*
FLOWERING *Once, with a few later* TYPE *Wichurana rambler*
SCENT *Light to medium musk, citrus* ZONES *5–9*

Also known as 'Direktör Benschop', the pure white flowers of this rose make it good for brightening up a shady spot. The flowers are semi-double, with prominent golden-yellow stamens that make them attractive to bees. They are set off by dark-green, healthy leaves. Also grows well on a sunny wall, pergola, or good-sized arch.

Chevy Chase

HEIGHT *13ft (4m)* SPREAD *10ft (3m)* FLOWERING *Once*
TYPE *Rambler* SCENT *Light or none* ZONES *6–9*

This is probably the best dark-crimson rambler, the small flowers being very neat and perfectly formed. They are produced profusely a little later than most roses, but then keep their color for a long time. It works well grown up a small tree or large shrub. An extremely healthy rose.

Leverkusen

HEIGHT *10ft (3m)* SPREAD *6ft (2m)* FLOWERING *Repeat*
TYPE *Climber* SCENT *Medium fruit* ZONES *5–10*

'Leverkusen' was introduced in 1954 and was the first of a group called the Kordesii Hybrids, bred for great winter hardiness and disease-resistance. It is still highly regarded today and has attractive, quite large, yellow flowers—deeper in color in the middle, much softer on the outside. They are followed by hips that stay green for a long time, eventually turning yellow. 'Leverkusen' makes a bushy climber tolerant of shade. It could also be grown as a large shrub.

'Chevy Chase'

'Veilchenblau'

Veilchenblau

HEIGHT *15ft (4.5m)* SPREAD *6ft (2m)*
FLOWERING *Single* TYPE *Rambler*
SCENT *Medium to strong fruity* ZONES *6–10*

'Veilchenblau' is the best known of a small group of ramblers (including 'Violette' and 'Bleu Magenta'), each having little flowers in shades of purple, this being the lightest. Color starts reddish-purple, changing to blue-violet, then gray-violet. With its large heads of flowers, it presents the range of colors at any one time. The stems are nearly thornless—not ideal for a rambler growing into a tree, since there is nothing for it to hook onto—but easier to train against a wall, pillar, or pergola. Thrives in many climates and tolerates shade well.

Climbing Etoile de Hollande

HEIGHT *13ft (4m)* SPREAD *8ft (2.5m)*
FLOWERING *Repeat* TYPE *Hybrid tea*
SCENT *Strong old rose* ZONES *6–10*

'Climbing Etoile de Hollande' is a versatile choice: as well as being suited to warm, sunny walls (p.171), it can also tolerate a relatively shady site. In fact, a north-facing wall can be beneficial choice for this rose, as the position can help to avoid the risk of the flowers burning if the sun gets too strong. A vigorous climber, with fragrant flowers that are a wonderful rich, velvety-crimson color; these can be a little formless when fully out, but a beautiful, classically old-hybrid-tea shape at first. Not the healthiest rose, but with care and attention, wonderful in the garden. Sets a good crop of large red hips if not dead-headed.

The Pilgrim

HEIGHT *10ft (3m)* SPREAD *6ft (2m)* FLOWERING *Repeat*
TYPE *David Austin climbing English rose*
SCENT *Medium tea and myrrh* CULTIVAR *'Auswalker'*
ZONES *5–10*

'The Pilgrim' has been growing on an open but north-facing wall at David Austin Roses for many years, and every year looks absolutely superb. It is pruned fairly lightly and has eventually reached right up to the gutters of a two-story building, although it could easily be kept shorter. The yellow flowers will brighten up any wall, the 140 petals being perfectly arranged in a rosette.

James Galway

HEIGHT *10ft (3m)* SPREAD *6ft (2m)* FLOWERING *Repeat*
TYPE *David Austin climbing English rose*
SCENT *Light to medium old rose* CULTIVAR *'Auscrystal'*
ZONES *5–11*

After initially being introduced as a shrub, it soon became evident that 'James Galway' is much better grown as a climber. It has large flowers tightly packed, with about 130 very weather-resistant petals. These are a lovely warm pink in the center, paling to blush at the edges. The stems have few thorns and are stiff, but can still be fanned out on a 6ft (2m) high wall or fence.

Climbing Madame Caroline Testout

HEIGHT *16ft (5m)* SPREAD *8ft (2.5m)*
FLOWERING *Some repeat* TYPE *Climbing hybrid tea*
SCENT *Medium sweet* ZONES *5–11*

With its large, silvery-pink, rather rounded flowers and rolled-back petals, 'Madame Caroline Testout' is a distinctive rose. Its growth is quite stiff and prickly—not the easiest to fan out. It's important, therefore, to give it a good-sized wall, 13–16ft (4–5m) high, to grow on. The flowers last a long time on the plant, but, luckily, the petals drop off cleanly. This climbing form originated from a bush that was planted in huge quantities along sidewalks in Portland, Oregon. It is healthy, tough, reliable, and extremely long-lived, often lasting 100 years or more.

'Climbing Etoile de Hollande'

'James Galway'

'The Pilgrim'

'Climbing Madame Caroline Testout'

'Charles de Mills'

Roses for cold, winter climates

While it is possible to protect roses in winter, if you know that your garden often experiences particularly harsh winters below 5°F (-15°C), it is so much easier to plant hardy varieties that don't mind the cold.

Blanc Double de Coubert

HEIGHT *5ft (1.5m)* SPREAD *5ft (1.5m)*
FLOWERING *Repeat* TYPE *Rugosa*
SCENT *Strong old rose* ZONES *3–9*

This is the best of the white rugosa hybrids. It is typically rugosa in appearance, and in terms of winter hardiness and health ranks highly. The flowers appear fully double at first, but open up to reveal the stamens. The fragrance is just like that of the true species, perhaps a little less strong, but nonetheless delicious. It produces a nice crop of large orange hips. A good choice for the back of a border. It's one fault is that the flowers spoil in the rain.

'Blanc Double de Coubert'

194

Charles de Mills

HEIGHT *4ft (1.2m)* SPREAD *5ft (1.5m)* FLOWERING *Single*
TYPE *Old rose Gallica* SCENT *Variable old rose* ZONES *4–9*

An easily recognizable rose thanks to the "sliced off"
appearance of its blooms, which start a rich crimson-purple,
before gradually turning pure purple. Their shape is initially
shallowly cupped, the petals eventually reflexing back
around the outside. The stems are nearly thornless and not
strong, so they can sag under the weight of the flowers. It is
best to accept this, since, with light pruning, they make an
attractive mound. Alternatively, grow them through another
shrub that will support the stems and make a lovely
combination. Fragrance is variable and normally light,
although it can be strong at the right time. A tough, mostly
healthy rose. Sometimes called 'Bizarre Triomphant'.

Thérèse Bugnet

HEIGHT *6ft (2m)* SPREAD *4ft (1.2m)* FLOWERING *Repeat*
TYPE *Rugosa* SCENT *Strong old rose* ZONES *3–9*

'Thérèse Bugnet' has rugosa hybrids on both sides of its
parentage, the seed parent being a cross with *R. acicularis*, one
of the hardiest of roses. That said, it is not obviously rugosa
in appearance—the leaves are fairly smooth, and it is nearly
thornless. The growth is upright, the loosely double, pure
rose-pink flowers produced mostly at the top. Worthy of
"normal" garden situations as well as tough ones. The similar
'Louis Bugnet' has red buds that open to pure white flowers.
Both are excellent planted as a hedge or in a mixed border.

The Lark Ascending

HEIGHT *6ft (2m)* SPREAD *5ft (1.5m)* FLOWERING *Repeat*
TYPE *David Austin English rose* SCENT *Light tea/musk*
CULTIVAR *'Ausursula'* ZONES *4–9*

Yellow- and apricot-colored roses are generally not hardy,
but there is always the exception that proves the rule. 'The
Lark Ascending' is one. It is very pretty, with semi-double,
open-cupped blooms produced in large heads that open in
sequence, giving a long flowering season. It makes a tall,
upright but bushy plant for hedging, backs of borders, or as
single specimens.

'Thérèse Bugnet'

'The Lark Ascending'

Rosa spinosissima 'Altaica'

HEIGHT *6ft (2m)* SPREAD *3ft (1m)*
FLOWERING *Single* TYPE *Wild rose*
SCENT *Strong musk* ZONES *3–8*

Rosa spinosissima, otherwise known as the 'Scots Rose' or 'Burnet Rose', is notable for its extreme toughness and hardiness. It is native to much of Europe, as far west as Iceland and east to Russia. It is characterized by small white flowers, small leaves, thorny stems, and black hips. 'Altaica' is a form that grows much taller than the original species, but retains its other characters and adds beautiful fall color. Superb fragrance.

Rosa alba 'Semiplena'

HEIGHT *8ft (2.5m)* SPREAD *6ft (2m)*
FLOWERING *Single* TYPE *Old rose Alba*
SCENT *Strong old rose* ZONES *3–9*

This is an ancient rose, dating to the 14th century, and may be the so-called 'White Rose of York'. Not only is it extremely winter-hardy, to temperatures as low as -40°F (-40°C), but it's also tough enough to survive decades of neglect. The medium-sized flowers are semi-double, pure white, with a large boss of rich yellow stamens much loved by bees. The fragrance is strong and delicious. Indeed, this rose is grown in Bulgaria to produce the essential oil attar of roses. It sets a crop of large, orange, dog-rose-shaped hips. The leaves are an attractive gray-green and generally healthy, although rust can be a problem late in the season. A versatile rose for the back of a border, a wild area, or a hedge.

Summer Wine

HEIGHT *12ft (3.6m)*
SPREAD *6ft (2m)*
FLOWERING *Repeat* TYPE *Climber*
SCENT *Medium* CULTIVAR *'Korizont'*
ZONES *5–9*

'Summer Wine' can be grown as a shrub or climber, depending on climate and pruning. In colder regions, it makes a fairly substantial shrub; in warmer ones, a lovely climber. It is valuable both for the beauty of its flowers and the wonderful crop of hips that follow them. The flowers are medium to large and officially semi-double, although they look single, with just eight to 10 petals. The buds are bright coral, opening to a soft salmon-pink with a yellow center. Standing out are the stamens, with crimson filaments and yellow anthers. The hips are large, rounded, and orange-red. A very tough rose.

John Davis

HEIGHT *8ft (2.5m)* SPREAD *6ft (2m)*
FLOWERING *Repeat* TYPE *Shrub*
SCENT *Light musk* ZONES *3–9*

One of the most winter-hardy roses available, 'John Davis' could even be hardy to Zone 2. It was the first of the 'Explorer' series bred by Svedja in Canada for cold winter areas. It has pretty, medium-sized, pure-pink flowers, rather like the old roses, and it repeat-flowers well. In a warmer climate, it makes a lovely short rambler; in colder climes, it will stay as an arching shrub.

Rosa pendulina

HEIGHT *6ft (2m)* SPREAD *5ft (1.5m)*
FLOWERING *Single* TYPE *Wild rose*
SCENT *Light or none* ZONES *3–9*

A wild rose native to the cold Alpine regions of central and southern Europe, it is also able to survive the very cold winters of North America. In tough conditions, it will stay quite short, barely more than 3ft (1m), but perhaps twice that height in gardens with temperate climates. The flowers are small, single, and a purplish pink. They are followed by bright-red, pear-shaped hips. Completely or very nearly thornless.

Country Dancer

HEIGHT *5ft (1.5m)* SPREAD *3ft (1m)*
FLOWERING *Repeat* TYPE *Shrub*
SCENT *Medium fruit* ZONES *4–9*

A Griffith Buck rose bred to survive the cold Iowa winters, 'Country Dancer' has the added, and not often encountered, advantage of growing and flowering well in shade. The large, semi-double flowers are a rich pink that fades slightly with age, and they have a good fruity fragrance. In cooler climates, and by pruning hard, it can be kept as a short shrub no more than 3ft (1m) tall, although it can be encouraged to twice that height. A tough rose that puts up with poor conditions, but worthy of a prominent spot and better conditions.

Roses for
arches, pergolas, obelisks & pillars

These structures are a great way to feature climbing roses within your garden. Arches need varieties that flower from the ground up and are flexible enough to be tied down to grow over them. Pergolas are good with a combination of climbers on their pillars and some ramblers that can be trained horizontally along the top. Upright, tall shrubs are good for pillars and obelisks.

'Narrow Water'

Narrow Water

HEIGHT *8ft (2.5m)* SPREAD *6ft (2m)* FLOWERING *Repeat*
TYPE *Climbing noisette* SCENT *Medium to strong musk*
ZONES *6–9*

The pretty little flowers are produced in great profusion right
to the end of the season. The pink buds open to semi-double
mauve blooms that fade to cream and white, giving a lovely
mix of colors. It has the musky clove fragrance typical
of noisettes. Good for growing over an arch, through
a small tree, or as a tall shrub if kept pruned. Unusually hardy
for a noisette.

Rural England

HEIGHT *10ft (3m)* SPREAD *8ft (2.5m)* FLOWERING *Repeat*
TYPE *Rambler* SCENT *Light* ZONES *6–10*

'Rural England' looks like a number of other ramblers, but
has the advantage of good repeat-flowering and not being
super vigorous. The medium-sized, soft-pink flowers are
produced in large bunches at the end of almost thornless
stems, making it easy to train and tie in. A lovely rose that can
also be grown as a large cascading shrub.

Malvern Hills

HEIGHT *13ft (4m)* SPREAD *10ft (3m)*
FLOWERING *Repeat* TYPE *David Austin English rose rambler*
SCENT *Light to medium musk* CULTIVAR *'Auscanary'*
ZONES *6–11*

A lovely and versatile rose. The abundant flowers are quite
small, turning from buff to yellow then cream. The petals are
in a rosette formation with, initially at least, a little button
eye. 'Malvern Hills' is vigorous enough to cover a pergola
quickly, but without becoming a menace.

'Rural England'

'Malvern Hills'

Paul Noël

HEIGHT *13ft (4m)* SPREAD *10ft (3m)* FLOWERING *Some repeating* TYPE *Rambler* SCENT *Medium tea/fruit* ZONES *6–9*

A rather unusual rambler resulting from an interesting cross between the wild rose *R. wichurana* and the tea rose 'Monsieur Tillier'. It was widely grown as 'Paul Transon' in the UK, until the confusion with the similar 'Paul Noël' was recognized. The large size and the color—soft salmon-pink, quickly paling—come from its tea parent. The first flowering in early summer is generous and is followed by a second flush later in the season, especially if the soil is kept damp. Its lax growth definitely comes from its wild rose background and makes it perfect for growing along pergolas or over outbuildings and trees. The fragrance is an interesting mix of apple with a hint of chrysanthemum.

Highwire Flyer

HEIGHT *6ft (2m)* SPREAD *3ft (1m)* FLOWERING *Repeat* TYPE *Rambler* SCENT *None* CULTIVAR *'Radwire'* ZONES *4–11*

Most obelisks are no more than 6ft (2m) tall, so this is a perfectly sized rose for an obelisk. The size makes it easy to care for and keep neat and tidy, just what is needed when it is in the middle of a border surrounded by other plants. Extremely healthy and winter-hardy. The large, 4in- (10cm-) diameter flowers are bright magenta-pink and produced freely.

'Highwire Flyer'

'Paul Noël'

'Purple Skyliner'

Purple Skyliner

HEIGHT *8ft (2.6m)* SPREAD *6ft (2m)*
FLOWERING *Repeat* TYPE *Climber* SCENT *Medium*
CULTIVAR *'Franwekpurp'* ZONES *6–9*

This is an excellent choice for an obelisk or pillar. Its height is just right, it flowers profusely and continuously, and it is very healthy. The semi-double, soft-purple flowers fade to gray and have a lovely fragrance. A tough variety, 'Purple Skyliner' tolerates some shade and poor conditions.

Climbing Pinkie

HEIGHT *10ft (3m)* SPREAD *6ft (2m)*
FLOWERING *Repeat* TYPE *Climber*
SCENT *Medium to strong*
ZONES *6–10*

An ideal rose for an arch. In warm climates, it is continuous and free-flowering; in cooler areas, it still has a long season. The individual flowers are semi-double and a pretty mid-pink, with a good to very good fruity fragrance. The stems are thornless and easily trained over whatever structure is offered. Or they can be left to become a superb heap of blooms.

Jasmina

HEIGHT *8ft (2.5m)* SPREAD *3ft (1m)*
FLOWERING *Repeat* TYPE *Climber*
SCENT *Strong fruity*
CULTIVAR *'Korcentex'* ZONES *5–11*

'Jasmina' is a lovely variety, with very double flowers, the petals being arranged in a quartered rosette like those of the old roses. They are medium-sized, varying in color between violet and pink, and have a strong and delicious fragrance—fresh apple with hints of pear and apricot. 'Jasmina' produces an abundance of flowers—which are good for cutting—and repeats well. It is a very winter-hardy variety and extremely healthy.

Crown Princess Margareta

HEIGHT *10ft (3m)* SPREAD *8ft (2.5m)*
FLOWERING *Repeat* TYPE *David Austin climbing English rose*
SCENT *Strong fruity*
CULTIVAR *'Auswinter'* ZONES *4–8*

A rose with wonderfully rich apricot flowers and a strong, fruity fragrance, although there is a hint of tea in there as well. The many petals are beautifully arranged in a rosette. While 'Crown Princess Margareta' can be kept as a large shrub, it is better trained as a climber, especially in warmer climates. Healthy and winter-hardy.

"Arches and pergolas work best when they serve a clear function in a garden, marking the transition from one area to the next."

Warm Welcome

HEIGHT *8ft (2.5m)*
SPREAD *5ft (1.5m)*
FLOWERING *Repeat*
TYPE *Patio climber* SCENT *Light*
CULTIVAR *'Chewizz'* ZONES *6–9*

A particularly vivid and eye-catching rose. It produces a mass of small, nearly single flowers of bright, bright orange. They are produced continuously the whole season long, and from the ground up to the top of the plant, until the cold stops them. It is a very healthy rose, and excellent for obelisks and pillars.

Open Arms

HEIGHT *8ft (2.5m)*
SPREAD *6ft (2m)*
FLOWERING *Repeat*
TYPE *Patio rambler*
SCENT *Light musk*
CULTIVAR *'Chewpixcel'*
ZONES *6–9*

The breeder of this rose, Chris Warner, introduced several varieties under the headings of Patio Climbers and Patio Ramblers. 'Open Arms' belonging to the latter. As the name suggests, its distinctive character is that it is short and compact, and, so, suitable for small spaces. Wonderfully, it flowers from the ground up. 'Open Arms' has small, semi-double flowers that open salmon-pink, turning pale pink with a central white eye and prominent stamens. It is healthy and flowers almost continuously through to cold weather. Stems are easy to train over an arch or fan out against a wall or fence.

Maid of Kent

HEIGHT *13ft (4m)*
SPREAD *10ft (3m)*
FLOWERING *Repeat*
TYPE *Climber* SCENT *Light*
ZONES *6–9*

'Maid of Kent' is one of those roses that could be called a climber or a rambler. It is a worthwhile variety, producing great quantities of small semi-double, soft-pink flowers that fade to blush. Its growth is vigorous and lax, making it perfect for pergolas and growing through trees.

'Peggy Martin'

Night Owl

HEIGHT *10ft (3m)* SPREAD *6ft (2m)*
FLOWERING *Repeat* TYPE *Climber* SCENT *Light*
CULTIVAR *'Wekpurosot'* ZONES *5–10*

A wonderfully deep-colored, distinctive rose. The flowers are large—4in (10cm) across—and nearly single. Their color is rich purple, with just the base of the petals turning white. They are produced regularly throughout the year, and, if not dead-headed, a fine crop of large, rounded, orange hips appear. With *Rosa soulieana* in its background, this variety's leaves are slightly grayish, setting off the color of the flowers even better.

'Night Owl'

Peggy Martin

HEIGHT *15ft (4.5m)* SPREAD *8ft (2.5m)*
FLOWERING *Some repeat* TYPE *Rambler*
SCENT *Light* ZONES *5–11*

Also known as the Hurricane Katrina rose, this is a tough variety and a great survivor. While 'Peggy Martin' can say how it came down through her family, its parentage is unknown. The flowers are small, in shades of pink, and prolifically produced, with an excellent first crop and more coming later in the year. It has lax growth, so perfect for training over a pergola or along a fence. Stems are thornless, although the undersides of the leaves are not.

Quicksilver

HEIGHT *6ft (2m)* SPREAD *3ft (1m)*
FLOWERING *Repeat* TYPE *Climber* SCENT *Light*
CULTIVAR *'Korpucoblu'* ZONES *5–9*

Its rich, lavender-mauve color and good-sized flowers make 'Quicksilver' stand out. It is the right vigor for anywhere in the garden where you want a short climber. Aside from a pillar or obelisk, it is also ideal for a fence or wall. A good cut flower that is healthy and winter-hardy.

Winner's Circle

HEIGHT *10ft (3m)* SPREAD *6ft (2m)* FLOWERING *Repeat*
TYPE *Climber* SCENT *Light or none* CULTIVAR *'Radwin'*
ZONES *4–10*

A rose that demands to be noticed! First, for the fire-engine red color of its almost-single flowers. Second, for its impressive health. Additionally, if not dead-headed, it sets a wonderful crop of bright-orange hips in the fall, when its leaves also turn burgundy. It is winter-hardy.

'Quicksilver'

'Winner's Circle'

205

Snow Goose

HEIGHT *8ft (2.5m)* SPREAD *3ft (1m)*
FLOWERING *Repeat* TYPE *David Austin English rose*
SCENT *Light musk* CULTIVAR *'Auspom'* ZONES *6–11*

A most charming, free-flowering variety. The flowers are small and produced freely and continuously over a long period. With its noisette background, it is happier in the generally warmer summers of North America than those of its home in the UK. The leaves are small, too—a pale green that sets off the white flowers well. The stems are very nearly thornless.

Laguna

HEIGHT *8ft (2.5m)* SPREAD *3ft (1m)*
FLOWERING *Repeat* TYPE *Climber*
SCENT *Strong fruity* CULTIVAR *'Koradigel'* ZONES *5–10*

A garden-worthy variety notable for its fragrance, which is particularly delicious and strong. It is a rich and well-balanced mix of different components, including fresh lemon, lychee, old rose, and patchouli! The large flowers (up to 4in/10cm across) are a pure, deep pink. 'Laguna' is an award-winning rose—healthy and extremely winter-hardy. It flowers well in part shade.

Cancan

HEIGHT *10ft (3m)* SPREAD *4ft (1.2m)*
FLOWERING *Repeat* TYPE *Climber* SCENT *Light*
CULTIVAR *'Radcancan'* ZONES *5–9*

'Cancan' is similar to 'American Pillar', but significantly shorter, and repeat-flowers well, so good for a medium-sized pergola, large arch, or for training along a fence. Like the 'Knock Outs' also bred by Bill Radler, it is healthy and hardy. The cup-shaped, semi-double flowers are magenta-red, paling to soft pink with a white eye.

The Albrighton Rambler

HEIGHT *13ft (4m)* SPREAD *10ft (3m)* FLOWERING *Repeat*
TYPE *David Austin English rose rambler*
SCENT *Light musk* CULTIVAR *'Ausmobile'* ZONES *5–11*

The individual flowers of this variety are like perfect, little old roses, with many petals beautifully arranged around a central darker eye. They are a soft pink (sometimes slightly apricot), paling to blush, then almost to white, and are held in large sprays on the end of long, gracefully arching stems. Not being too vigorous and with a fairly lax habit, it is quite easy to train this rose horizontally over a pergola.

'Snow Goose'

'Cancan'

'Laguna'

'The Albrighton Rambler'

Roses for
walls & fences

A rose on a wall or fence is one of the absolute classic
garden elements. With the right variety choice, they
can give more than any other type of climber—beautiful
blooms, color, scent, and a long flowering period. They
can turn a drab wall into a beautiful one.

'Nahema'

Nahema

HEIGHT *12ft (3.6m)* SPREAD *6ft (2m)* FLOWERING *Repeat*
TYPE *Climber* SCENT *Medium to strong* CULTIVAR *'Deléri'*
ZONES *5–9*

The flowers of 'Nahema' are in the classic style of old roses,
full-petaled and quartered. They are pink, about 4in (10cm)
across, and have a delicious fruity fragrance—a combination
of peach and citrus. For walls and fences, it is always wise to
choose varieties that aren't too vigorous, otherwise they can
be difficult to manage. 'Nahema' fits the bill.

Garden Sun

HEIGHT *10ft (3m)* SPREAD *6ft (2m)* FLOWERING *Repeat*
TYPE *Climber* SCENT *Light* CULTIVAR *'Melvaleir'*
ZONES *6–9*

'Garden Sun' is a good name for this golden-yellow rose. The
flowers are not unlike the classic old-climber 'Gloire de
Dijon', with a similar petal arrangement and the color being
a pleasing mix of yellow, apricot, and the occasional bit
of pink. It copes well with the heat and is pretty as a cut rose.
A healthy variety.

Claire Austin

HEIGHT *10ft (3m)* SPREAD *6ft (2m)* FLOWERING *Repeat*
TYPE *David Austin climbing English rose* SCENT *Strong myrrh*
CULTIVAR *'Ausprior'* ZONES *5–11*

Like red roses, good white roses are not easy to breed. 'Claire
Austin', though, has large flowers and excellent health. It was
first introduced as a shrub rose, but its vigor soon made it
plain that it is best grown as a short climber. The rounded,
creamy-white flowers have a strong and delicious myrrh
fragrance, with additional hints of meadowsweet, heliotrope,
and vanilla.

'Garden Sun'

'Claire Austin'

Open Arms

HEIGHT *8ft (2.5m)*
SPREAD *6ft (2m)*
FLOWERING *Repeat*
TYPE *Patio rambler*
SCENT *Light musk*
CULTIVAR *'Chewpixcel'*
ZONES *6–9*

The breeder of this rose, Chris Warner, introduced various patio climbers and patio ramblers. All are relatively short and compact, and so suitable for small spaces. They also have the wonderful ability to flower from the ground up. 'Open Arms' has small, almost single flowers that open salmon-pink, turning to pale pink, with a central white eye and a prominent bunch of stamens. It is very healthy and flowers almost continuously through to the cold weather. The stems, being flexible, are easy to fan out against a wall or fence.

Sombreuil

HEIGHT *12ft (4m)*
SPREAD *6ft (2m)*
FLOWERING *Repeat*
TYPE *Climbing tea*
SCENT *Strong tea* ZONES *6-11*

A wonderful rose, especially in the drier parts of the country. It is meant to be a tea rose, but looking at the flowers, it is hard to see that association, as they are very full-petaled, with many petals neatly arranged in a flat, but beautiful, flower. The fragrance is strong and tealike. The flowers can spoil in wet weather, but they are superb in drier parts. Also known as 'Old Colonial White'.

Bathsheba

HEIGHT *10ft (3m)*
SPREAD *6ft (2m)*
FLOWERING *Repeat*
TYPE *David Austin climbing*
English rose SCENT *Strong myrrh*
CULTIVAR *'Auschimbley'* ZONES *5–10*

This rose makes a strong impression in the garden. It is the perfect size for a wall or fence, where it can easily be kept under control, and its flowers can easily be accessed for their scent and for cutting. The flowers are 4in (10cm) or more across and have about 170 beautifully arranged petals. Their fragrance is superb, a delicious floral myrrh with hints of tea and honey. They are a beautiful blend of subtle apricot-pink and soft yellow, paling to cream on the outer petals. A healthy rose that repeat-flowers well.

Lady of Shalott

HEIGHT *10ft (3m)*
SPREAD *6ft (2m)*
FLOWERING *Repeat*
TYPE *David Austin English rose*
SCENT *Medium to strong tea and fruit*
CULTIVAR *'Ausnyson'* ZONES *5–9*

A versatile and beautiful rose, and one of the best of the English roses. It is normally grown as a substantial shrub (p.97), but it will quickly cover a 6–10ft- (2–3m-) high wall or fence, especially in warmer climates. The flowers are produced almost continuously from late spring/early summer until late in the year and, given a good spell of weather, a few flowers will open up in winter; these are ideal for bringing into the house. The unopened buds are a rich orange-red, opening to apricot. They have a delicious fragrance, a soft tea with hints of spiced apple and cloves. A very healthy rose.

Wollerton Old Hall

HEIGHT *10ft (3m)*
SPREAD *6ft (2m)*
FLOWERING *Repeat*
TYPE *David Austin climbing*
English rose SCENT *Strong myrrh*
CULTIVAR *'Ausblanket'* ZONES *5–10*

'Wollerton Old Hall' is remarkable for the strength of its fragrance and the size of its flowers. It is a healthy, fairly vigorous variety, and so needs a good-sized wall or fence to grow on, although the stems aren't too stiff, so it can be fanned out quite easily. The unopened buds have flashes of red on the outside, the flowers opening to the softest pale apricot before paling a little with age. They are beautifully rounded, the central stamens rarely showing themselves, although still easily accessible to bees. The fragrance is a particularly strong, warm myrrh with hints of citrus, although some say magnolia.

'Guirlande d'Amour'

Guirlande d'Amour

HEIGHT *8ft (2.5m)* SPREAD *6ft (2m)*
FLOWERING *Repeat* TYPE *Climbing hybrid musk*
SCENT *Strong* CULTIVAR *'Lenalbi'* ZONES *5–9*

'Guirlande d'Amour' produces a mass of pure white flowers in huge pyramids of up to 80 blooms. Its flowers are semi-double, with stamens in full view, giving off a strong, musky, clove fragrance, typical of this group of roses. It can also be grown as a beautiful, arching shrub. A healthy and reliable rose.

Gertrude Jekyll

HEIGHT *8ft (2.5m)* SPREAD *6ft (2m)*
FLOWERING *Repeat* TYPE *David Austin English rose*
SCENT *Strong old rose* CULTIVAR *'Ausbord'*
ZONES *4–9*

'Gertrude Jekyll' is well-known for the strength of its classic old-rose fragrance. Not only that, but the large, pure, rich-pink flowers are beautiful, the many petals arranged in the shape of a rosette. With its fragrance, this rose should be planted where the flowers are easily accessible, perhaps by a door, on a wall that is close to a favorite path, or on an arch.

'Gertrude Jekyll'

Roses for growing through trees

It is the natural habit of many wild roses to scramble up trees—that is what their thorns are for. A rambler tumbling through a big tree is a magnificent sight, and smaller trees can also look charming with more compact roses through them.

'Kew Rambler'

Kew Rambler

HEIGHT *16ft (5m)* SPREAD *10ft (3m)* FLOWERING *Once*
TYPE *Rambler* SCENT *Strong musk* ZONES *7–9*

One of the parents of 'Kew Rambler' is *Rosa soulieana*, a rarely seen climbing species with small creamy flowers, gray foliage, and many thorns. 'Kew Rambler' has inherited the last two characteristics, but its flowers are bigger and quite a bright pink with a white eye. In the fall, there is a good crop of small orange hips.

Francis E. Lester

HEIGHT *16ft (5m)* SPREAD *10ft (3m)* FLOWERING *Once*
TYPE *Rambler* SCENT *Strong musk* ZONES *6–9*

This is a wonderfully free-flowering rambler, the small single flowers being produced in large heads. They are a gentle, soft pink, paling to white in the center, the whole flower eventually turning that color. The petals drop cleanly (important in a rambler when the great majority of blooms will be out of reach) and are followed by an abundance of small orange-red hips that last well into the winter until the birds feast on them. The fragrance is the classic musk-type found in ramblers, which wafts on the wind, making it perceptible from some distance away. 'Francis E. Lester' can also be trained on pergolas, where its flowers will be more in reach. Altogether a healthy, tough, beautiful, and garden-worthy rose.

Rosa filipes 'Kiftsgate'

HEIGHT *40ft (12m) or more* SPREAD *26ft (8m) or more*
FLOWERING *Once* TYPE *Rambling species rose*
SCENT *Strong musk* ZONES *6–9*

Not a rose for the fainthearted—this is the most vigorous of all varieties. The one growing at Kiftsgate Court (after which it was named) is at least 80ft (25m) tall, growing up a copper beech tree. If space can be found, it is distinctive and beautiful. It has pale bronze-green young leaves. The individual flowers are white, quite small, but borne in huge, airy clusters of 100 or more and emit a delicious musk fragrance. They are followed by beautiful and long-lasting small rose-red hips. It can be grown in other situations, but will send out 10–13ft (3-4m) shoots each year and needs a lot of management.

'Francis E. Lester'

Rosa filipes 'Kiftsgate'

215

Gardenia

HEIGHT *15ft (4.5m)* SPREAD *10ft (3m)*
FLOWERING *Single* TYPE *Rambler* SCENT *Light to
medium musk* ZONES *6–9*

The early ramblers were crosses between assorted
climbing roses and garden roses. Rosa wichurana was a
popular choice, as it has lovely lax growth and repeat-
flowers a little. 'Gardenia' is a cross between this species
and the tea rose 'Perle des Jardins'. Introduced in 1899,
it was notable for two reasons—it was the first of the
large flowered ramblers, and it was yellow (a soft yellow
that quickly fades to cream and white, especially in the
heat). It is not too vigorous. Suitable for medium-sized
trees and doesn't swamp smaller ones.

Rambling Rector

HEIGHT *26ft (8m)* SPREAD *16ft (5m)* FLOWERING *Once*
TYPE *Rambler* SCENT *Strong musk* ZONES *6–9*

A vigorous rose, 'Rambling Rector' is better suited to
growing through trees than to being trained against a
wall, where it will soon become a difficult-to-manage
monster. It will grow up through the branches, hanging
on by its many thorns, and producing long, strongly
fragrant festoons of small, semi-double, pure-white
flowers. These are soon followed by small orange hips
that last into the winter and are eventually taken by the
birds. 'Rambling Rector' needs a large tree such as an
oak, beech, or ash (it can easily swallow up and kill
smaller ones). Rather surprisingly, it can also be grown
as a large weeping standard, although this needs plenty
of space and stout staking.

Climbing Cécile Brunner

HEIGHT *26ft (8m)* SPREAD *13ft (4m)* FLOWERING *Once*
TYPE *Climber* SCENT *Medium sweet* ZONES *5–9*

A mature plant of the climbing form of 'Cécile Brunner'
in full flower is a sight not easily forgotten. The
abundance of flowers is breathtaking, each bud like a
miniature hybrid tea with scrolled petals. As the buds
open up, they form a rosette shape with a button eye,
and the color fades from clear pink to blush. It is
essentially a once-flowering rose, but a few later flowers
are produced. This climbing form originated from the
original 'Cécile Brunner', which is only about 3ft (1m)
tall and repeat-flowers very well—otherwise it
is identical.

White Climbing Maman Cochet

HEIGHT *15ft (4.5m)* SPREAD *10ft (3m)*
FLOWERING *Repeat* TYPE *Tea climber*
SCENT *Medium to strong tea* ZONES *7–11*

In a warm climate, this flowers continuously year-
round, a rarity for a rose vigorous enough to grow into
trees. It requires a good degree of warmth to do its best,
and, if growing happily, can swamp small trees, so
needs to be placed with care. In cooler climates, it is still
worthwhile for smaller trees and for fences, walls, and
obelisks. The flowers are large and long and hang
downward—an advantage in a climbing rose. Their
color is lemon yellow, with streaks of pink on the outer
petals. It is a sport from the 'White Maman Cochet',
which itself sported from the original 'Maman Cochet'.

'Gardenia'

'Climbing Cécile Brunner'

'Rambling Rector'

'White Climbing Maman Cochet'

'Treasure Trove'

Rosa banksiae 'Lutea'

Treasure Trove

HEIGHT *33ft (10m)* SPREAD *16ft (5m)* FLOWERING *Once*
TYPE *Rambler* SCENT *Medium sweet* ZONES *7–9*

The original seedling of this was found in the garden of
Mr. John Treasure below a 'Kiftsgate' rose and near a
'Buff Beauty', and so it is supposed that they are the two
parents. It certainly has the extreme vigor of 'Kiftsgate',
and the medium-sized apricot flowers are reminiscent
of 'Buff Beauty'. They fade with age and sometimes
become quite pink in the heat. The young leaves are
particularly richly colored and a lovely feature, as are
the medium-sized, rounded red hips that last well into
late winter. There is no variety with the same vigor that
is similar in appearance.

Rosa banksiae 'Lutea'

HEIGHT *23ft (7m)* SPREAD *10ft (3m)* FLOWERING *Once*
TYPE *Rambling species rose* SCENT *Light* ZONES *8–11*

If, in spring, you spot a vigorous climber with an
abundance of small bright-yellow flowers, it is likely
to be *Rosa banksiae* 'Lutea', also known as 'Lady Banks'
Rose'. It is extremely free-flowering and the color is a
delight to the eye at that time of year. It is best suited
to a Mediterranean climate; in the UK, it can get cut
back if there is a really hard frost, although it still
performs well. It has no thorns at all, and so apparently
nothing to keep it attached to a tree, but it will still
successfully scramble through them, and is easier to
manage like this than on most walls. The single white
form, *R. banksiae* var. *normalis*, has the most wonderful
violet fragrance; unfortunately, only faint in 'Lutea'.

'Hiawatha'

Hiawatha

HEIGHT *13ft (4m)* SPREAD *8ft (2.5m)*
FLOWERING *Single* TYPE *Rambler*
SCENT *Light or none* ZONES *5–9*

A not too vigorous rambler that will liven up a tree. The flowers are small, but produced freely in large heads. The base of the petal is white, the rest a rich crimson. This is a good choice for a medium-sized tree or a large arch, if careful management of the long stems is practiced.

"A rose-covered tree is a splendid sight, with masses of flowers hanging down in large, fragrant garlands."

ROSE care

Giving your roses the best start

The two fundamentals for healthy, free-flowering roses in the garden are to choose a variety that is tough, reliable, and disease-resistant, and then to prepare the ground well and plant it well. For the first, take a look at the Rose Selector (pp.86–219); for the second, read on.

Bare-root or container-grown?

Having selected a variety, you have the option of buying it either dormant, with no soil attached (known as "bare-root"), or as an actively growing, often flowering plant in a container. So, which should you choose?

There is a much wider range of varieties available as bare-root plants via mail order from nurseries, but they are only available from early winter through to mid-spring. They are dug from the field and are cheap, easy, and environmentally friendly to dispatch, making a small, light package. Since they have no leaves, they suffer little or no stress from being transplanted, although it's crucial that the roots not be allowed to dry out at any time between receipt and planting. If you can't plant the rose right away, perhaps because it's frosty or too wet, it's best to quickly "heel it in"—dig a hole just large enough to bury the roots and the bottom 2in (5cm) of the stem, firming the soil back around them. The rose should be happy like this for several weeks, if necessary.

Containerized roses are available year round, both from garden centers and via mail order. They require a plastic pot, potting compost, and several months of watering and general care before they are ready for sale, and delivery involves large boxes and couriers. If you're buying in person, check that the plant looks healthy and well cared-for. A containerized rose in flower will make an immediate effect in your garden, but it will need extra care and attention to thrive after the stress of being transplanted.

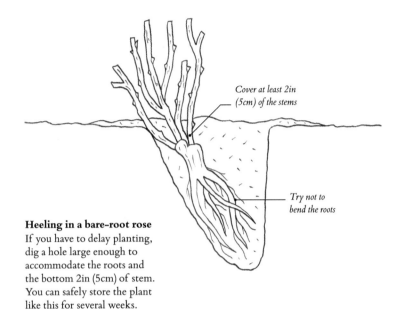

Cover at least 2in (5cm) of the stems

Try not to bend the roots

Heeling in a bare-root rose
If you have to delay planting, dig a hole large enough to accommodate the roots and the bottom 2in (5cm) of stem. You can safely store the plant like this for several weeks.

Getting the position right

As long as good, tough varieties are chosen, roses are generally not too fussy about where they are planted, provided they get at least five or six hours of full sun a day during the summer. (There are some exceptions: shade-tolerant roses, for instance, will manage with only three or four hours of full sun a day; see pp.188–193.) In hot climates, roses may benefit from being shaded from the ravages of the afternoon sun. If the site is wind-swept, choose varieties that can cope well with this, for example, the *Rosa spinosissima* and *Rosa rugosa* hybrids.

Planting at the foot of a wall, especially a south- or east-facing wall that's sheltered from the prevailing wind and rain, offers an extra challenge, since the soil is likely to be very dry. There needs to be at least 18in (50cm) depth of good soil, which doesn't sit on solid rock or foundations. Make the planting hole as big as you can and incorporate extra organic matter into the soil to retain moisture. If the site is underneath the overhang of a roof, you'll need to plant a short distance away from the wall, where the rain will reach the rose. An occasional deep soaking and the generous use of an annual mulch will help to conserve moisture, although it is important to do this before the rose shows signs of stress.

Excessive competition at the roots from trees and hedges can be a problem, especially while roses are getting established. If there are a lot of roots, it's best to plant farther away or to cut the other plant's roots back to give the rose's roots extra growing space. Ramblers and species roses generally cope better and will grow well despite being planted at the foot of trees, although they may need a year or two to get established.

Make sure there's enough room for your chosen rose. Use the height and spread information given in pp.86–219 as a guide for planting distances. If you're planting a hedge, plant them half their width apart.

Preparing the ground

Roses need a moisture-retentive soil that never becomes water-logged. Provided that the soil is neither heavy clay nor free-draining and sandy, it should be suitable for rose-growing. That being said, all soils can be improved by incorporating well-rotted organic matter when you plant, and mulching regularly from then on. This will help with moisture retention and will feed all the myriad organisms that are so important to the health of the soil and the plants growing in it. The pH (acidity/alkalinity) of the soil should ideally be around neutral (pH 7), although anything between 6 and 7.5 will be fine. It is worthwhile spending time and, if necessary, money trying to ensure the soil is as suitable as possible for the rose *before* planting. Once planted, improving the soil at root level is very difficult.

The organic matter can be in the form of homemade compost or animal manure, but both must be well rotted, otherwise the rotting process will use up nitrogen and starve the rose. Buying some soil improver—generally a blend of animal manure and plant waste, which should be well rotted and free of both viable weed seeds and living weeds—may be easiest. Homemade compost and manures are often full of weed material and can create a lot of extra work. Whatever organic matter one uses, it shouldn't be added to excess—one or two shovelfuls per planting hole, mixed in with the excavated soil, is adequate, as long as the soil is reasonably good. Poorer soils benefit from a bit more, but don't add more than about a quarter extra: it's liable to rot down and disappear, causing the soil level to dip and the soil to shrink away from the roots. Species roses and other once-flowering types will often be fine with little or no improvement to the soil.

Replacing a rose

If you want to plant where a rose has been growing, you'll need to do some extra preparation to avoid the risk of replant disease, whose symptoms are poor growth and slow establishment of the new rose. Often this is simply due to the soil being worn out—perhaps it hasn't been mulched for years or is compacted and devoid of the soil-borne organisms that are vital for strong growth. If the soil where the previous rose was growing looks in good heart—easy to dig, with plenty of worms and other creatures in it—then you can just prepare and plant as normal, and the new rose will grow away, especially if you apply mycorrhizal fungi at planting time.

If you suspect the soil is worn out, the fastest option, if you only want to plant a few roses, is to change the soil for each plant in a hole 18 x 18in (50 x 50cm) square and just as deep. It is important to be very fussy about the replacement soil—bought-in soil is often free-draining, has little or no organic matter, a high pH, and lacks structure—all characteristics that roses do not like. For one or two roses, this is not too much work, but for a bed with, say, twenty, it is a more serious undertaking. The alternative is to add generous quantities of well-rotted organic matter and grow a cover crop like the pretty, blue-flowered *Phacelia tanacetifolia* for two or three years before planting the new roses. This needs to be sown directly into the soil in the spring and dug in once it's finished flowering.

Preparing and planting the rose

The roots of bare-root roses should never be allowed to dry out. They should be kept in their original packaging in a cool, frost-free place, or heeled in if necessary (pp.222–223). Take them out an hour or two before you want to plant them and plunge them in a bucket of water until you have a hole ready to plant them in.

The compost of container-grown roses is often dry and difficult to re-wet once the rose is in the ground. If you plant it like this, the rose is likely to suffer from stress, take longer to get established, and be more vulnerable to pests and diseases. It is crucial, therefore, to soak it thoroughly by submerging the whole container in water for an hour or so before you're ready to plant, and then allowing it to drain. If, when you remove it from the pot, the roots form a solid mass and are circling around (that is, the rose was rootbound), they should be broken up and disentangled to encourage them to spread into the surrounding soil.

The hole you dig should be wide enough to accommodate the roots without bending them over and deep enough that the bud union—the point of attachment of the green shoots to the brown roots—is about 2in (5cm) below ground.

While the roots are wet, it's a good idea to sprinkle powdered mycorrhizal fungi on them. These fungi help plants extract water and nutrients from the soil, and there is evidence they can help roses to establish and to grow better in poor soils. The only time they can be applied is when planting, since they need to be in direct contact with the roots. It's a good idea to hold the rose over the planting hole while sprinkling them, so that any excess that doesn't stick to the roots is not wasted.

Check that the rose is at the right depth in the hole, with the point where the roots attach to the top-growth 2in (5cm) below ground level. Backfill with the soil and organic matter mix and firm in well, although not excessively. Water the newly planted rose, especially if the soil is at all dry. If it was container-grown, it will definitely need generous watering straight after planting, and also for the next few months if it's in full leaf and you plant it in the summer.

Transplanting

Roses can be transplanted successfully even if several years old. Small varieties are the easiest to move: they should be fine at ten years old, but a big rambler with extensive roots would be a real struggle to re-establish after as little as five years. Dig the rose up in winter and plant it immediately— dig the hole first! If there's any delay at all, keep the roots moist in a bucket of water or else heel the rose in until you can plant it properly.

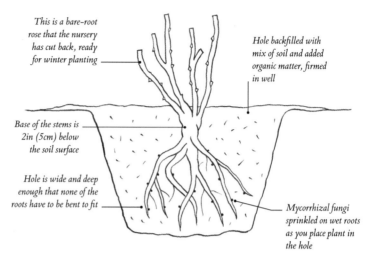

This is a bare-root rose that the nursery has cut back, ready for winter planting

Hole backfilled with mix of soil and added organic matter, firmed in well

Base of the stems is 2in (5cm) below the soil surface

Hole is wide and deep enough that none of the roots have to be bent to fit

Mycorrhizal fungi sprinkled on wet roots as you place plant in the hole

Planting a rose
Soak both bare-root and container-grown roses for an hour or so before you plant them, and water well immediately afterward.

Care in the first year

Bare-root roses will not need much extra watering in the first year unless the soil becomes very dry. Container-grown roses, though, will need regular watering. Make a low wall of soil, about 2ft (60cm) in diameter, around each rose to prevent the water from escaping.

Make sure you maintain a clear space around each rose, especially for the first year or two. Ideally, mulch for a square yard (meter) around it to help retain moisture and feed the soil, and keep that area free of weeds and encroaching plants.

Growing roses in containers

For most shrub roses, the container needs to be at least 18in (50cm) in diameter and the same in depth. Climbers require more space—at least 2ft (60cm) wide and deep. The bigger the container, the greater the availability of water and nutrients, thus reducing the risk of the rose running out of either.

You can fill your pot with a good-quality, peat-free potting compost or homemade garden compost that's completely rotted and free of perennial weeds, mixed 50:50 with good-quality soil. The soil will help with long-term nutrient supply and will retain water, while the compost will help to aerate the mix. The soil also adds weight, which will help to prevent the pot blowing over, especially if it's plastic. It's a good idea to raise the container up on pot feet, to ensure that it doesn't sit in water in wet weather.

Roses growing in pots need regular and generous watering. It is important to assess the moisture levels in the pot by digging down 6in (15cm) or so. The potting mix often contracts when dry, so that the water runs down the sides of it and straight out the bottom of the pot. If this happens, a spell of frequent watering will be necessary to re-wet it.

Propagating roses

In order to produce roses in bulk, commercial growers propagate roses by budding or grafting, where a single vegetative bud of the variety is carefully inserted under the bark of a rootstock and covered up. In midwinter, once it has knitted in place, the rootstock above the bud is cut off, which stimulates the growth of the grafted bud.

Since this process is a skilled operation and requires a suitable rootstock, grafting is best left to the experts. Home gardeners can instead propagate their roses by taking cuttings. This technique works for most varieties, although some roses are rather reluctant and others will refuse altogether.

The best time to take cuttings is from summer through to the fall, when it should be easy to find a stem that is semi-ripe and still has some flexibility and has recently flowered. The cutting should be about 6–8in (15–20cm) long. Since roots can emerge from anywhere along the stem, it doesn't matter how close to a bud you cut. Remove the growing tip, including any soft growth beneath it and all but two or three upper leaves. Insert each cutting to half its length, either into the ground in a sheltered position, or in a pot filled with peat-free seed and cutting compost in a shady spot in a greenhouse or cold frame. Water the cuttings well and continue to keep the compost moist. Once your cuttings are growing strongly and have a good root system—which can take from a few weeks to a year, depending on how warm it is—they can be moved to a more open nursery bed or potted on. Don't be tempted to try and move them too soon: the young roots are very delicate.

An alternative propagation method, suitable for varieties whose stems can be easily bent down to the ground (such as ramblers and ground-cover roses), is known as layering. This simply means cutting partway through a stem, burying it a little, and pegging it in place. After a year or so, roots should have formed, and the rooted stem can be cut from the parent plant and transplanted.

Seed collected from garden-grown roses will turn out differently from its parent plant, due to insects cross-pollinating varieties. Unfortunately, the results are nearly always much worse, but it can be fun to grow the seed and see what results. It should be taken from ripe hips and kept in a plastic bag in a fridge for two months before sowing. Once sown, keep in a warm, light place but below 60°F (15°C), since higher temperatures can inhibit germination. This is how new varieties are created, although many tens of thousands of seeds are usually required to find a single garden-worthy rose.

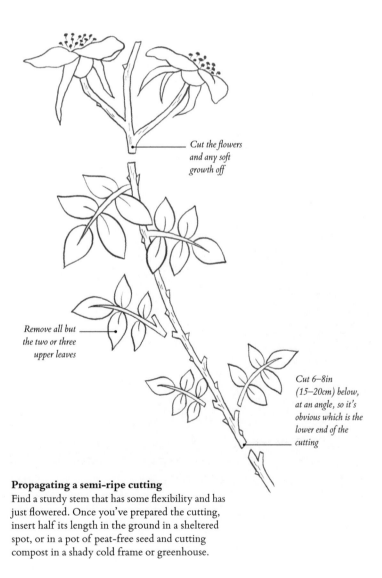

Cut the flowers and any soft growth off

Remove all but the two or three upper leaves

Cut 6–8in (15–20cm) below, at an angle, so it's obvious which is the lower end of the cutting

Propagating a semi-ripe cutting
Find a sturdy stem that has some flexibility and has just flowered. Once you've prepared the cutting, insert half its length in the ground in a sheltered spot, or in a pot of peat-free seed and cutting compost in a shady cold frame or greenhouse.

Looking after your roses

Once established, species roses and their hybrids can be left to their own devices, but most other types will benefit from a little more regular care.

Weeding & mulching

It's important for the health of your roses to keep the area immediately around them free of competition, so check regularly for any encroaching plants, whether weeds or vigorous neighbors outgrowing their space, and remove them. This will also ensure good air flow, which helps to reduce fungal infections.

To grow well, roses (and indeed all plants) need the soil to be in good condition. The best way to keep it that way is by regular mulching. A thick layer of mulch protects the soil from the elements, buries diseased leaves, helps with moisture retention and weed control, and prevents compaction. Most importantly, it encourages the proliferation of the myriad organisms that keep the soil healthy.

Mulch is simply a layer of organic matter that is applied to the top of the soil. It doesn't need to be particularly well rotted, since it stays on the surface. As long as it's free of weeds, it can consist of bark or wood chips, manure, garden compost, old potting compost, or spent mushroom compost (only if the soil is below pH 7, as it is quite alkaline). The material shouldn't be too fine or it may create a waterproof barrier.

The best time to apply a mulch is soon after pruning (pp.233–238), as there will be room to get in between the plants without knocking off young shoots. Spread the material in a layer 2–4in (5–10cm) thick, and, if necessary, top off any thin areas throughout the year.

Watering

While roses will survive long periods of drought, to grow well and produce plenty of long-lasting flowers, they need moisture at their roots. The amount of watering you'll need to do will depend on the weather and how free-draining your soil is. The best way to assess moisture levels is to dig a little hole about 6–8in (15–20cm) deep from time to time. If the base feels dry or not particularly moist, soak them well. It is always better to water occasionally but thoroughly, to encourage deep roots. While an automatic drip-irrigation system can be helpful, it needs careful monitoring to check that it's not either making the soil waterlogged or only damping the surface of the soil.

It's important to avoid splashing water on leaves, as this encourages many diseases. If you use a sprinkler system or can't avoid wetting the leaves with your hose, it's best to water your roses a little before the warmest point of the day, as this will help the leaves to dry out quickly. Early morning or evening watering, conversely, will result in leaves staying wet for a number of hours, increasing the chance of disease.

Feeding

While feeding roses is not essential, most varieties will benefit—especially those that have a long flowering period, which can drain the plants of energy. Any granular fertilizer with a nitrogen:phosphorus:potassium (NPK) ratio of around 5:5:10 will work well—the extra potassium supports flower production. Avoid those with a higher proportion of nitrogen (N), since they'll encourage lots of soft growth that will be less able to hold up a crop of flowers, while being more susceptible to pests and diseases.

The first feed should coincide with the start of strong spring growth, with a second one at the time of the first flush of flowers. A third application may be helpful in late summer, although no later, as it can encourage soft young growth at a time when it will be more susceptible to frost damage. Never apply more than the recommended amount, since this can do more harm than good. Scatter the granules around evenly in the area under the bush and water them in well if no rain is forecast.

Spraying or watering the leaves with a foliar feed may make them more resistant to disease. Seaweed-based ones seem to be particularly effective, as are those made with comfrey or nettles (although they're incredibly smelly).

Species roses and their near hybrids will usually not need any feeding, and once-flowering roses should be fine with just one application in spring.

Snap off the first flowers to die

Once all the flowers have died, cut the whole head off above a full leaf (one with at least five leaflets)

Dead-heading
Snap off individual flowers as they die, then cut off the whole flower-head just above the first full leaf. A new flower-head should grow from a dormant bud between this leaf and the stem.

Dead-heading

Regularly removing spent flowers keeps the rose looking good and encourages more flowers. This is particularly important if the petals don't drop off cleanly, leaving the rose covered with decaying flowers. Each bloom can be removed as it dies simply by snapping it off. Once all blooms on a head are spent, cut it back to the first full leaf (one that has five or seven leaflets) with pruning shears. Don't dead-head too late in the season, as this can encourage soft new growth that will be more susceptible to frost damage.

Once-flowering varieties don't need dead-heading unless they look unattractive. Roses grown for their hips, whether once- or repeat-flowering, shouldn't be dead-headed. If you're reluctant to lose the later flowers, you could experiment with only removing half the heads; or try dead-heading until late summer, and see if the hips still ripen in the remaining time.

Pruning and training

Much has been written about how to prune roses, with many supposedly important rules and regulations about what one should or shouldn't do. All this has made what is a relatively simple task into a seemingly very complicated one.

Many of the rules and regulations are left over from the time when roses were grown for exhibition purposes. They are for gardeners who were trying to grow the perfect bloom for the show bench, using varieties that bear little resemblance to the great majority of roses we grow today.

You prune a rose to create an attractively shaped plant that will flower as much, and as beautifully, as possible. Pruning can also keep the rose within the space you want it to fill, and help limit pests and diseases that overwinter on leaves and some older stems. Thinning out the main stems encourages good air flow and stimulates healthy new growth.

Pruning different types of roses

Given the wide variety of shapes and growth habits in roses, it's no surprise that each type is best suited to a particular pruning method. That said, it's worth remembering that supposedly bad pruning will never do any permanent damage to the rose. You'll build your confidence from year to year by trial-and-error and observation.

Repeat-flowering shrub roses, along with climbers and ramblers, are perhaps the most common rose types grown by home gardeners. As such, I've offered more detailed pruning tips for them on pp.234–235. For other varieties, read on.

Species roses and their hybrids

These shouldn't be pruned at all. They've grown happily, unpruned, for millions of years; pruning would spoil their shape and reduce the number of flowers and hips they produce. At most, you may need to remove the odd big woody stem at the base after a decade or two of growth, to rejuvenate the plant.

Once-flowering and tea roses

Although these can be pruned the same way as repeat-flowering shrub roses, there is a good argument for treating the once-flowering roses (essentially the gallicas, damasks, albas, centifolias, and mosses) slightly differently. These old roses have a different character to the repeat-flowerers, which can easily be lost if they are over-pruned. A light pruning, reducing their height by perhaps a quarter and leaving some wayward stems, will help to retain that character. Cut out any diseased or rubbing stems, but don't be tempted to thin or tidy them up too much.

Tea roses can flower more or less continuously, and resent being pruned too much. Once the bush is a few years old, simply cut out one or two of the least-productive stems each year to encourage fresh new growth from the base.

Hybrid teas and floribundas

These may need pruning a little harder than other shrub roses (see below) to help maintain their shape and to prevent them from growing lanky. If you want them to produce bigger flowers on stronger stems (like those exhibited in flower shows), you can prune them much harder, but this will weaken the plants and shorten their life span.

Standard roses

These should be pruned somewhat harder than you would the same variety grown without the long stem, since if the top is allowed to get too big it will be top-heavy and likely to break or be blown over. Shape it to encourage a spherical head.

Repeat-flowering shrub roses

At its simplest, pruning shrub roses (that is, all roses that aren't species roses, climbers, or ramblers) can just mean reducing the height of the rose by about half, depending on how tall you want the rose to be in that position. The harder the prune, the shorter (and more lenient) the plant. For better results, however, it is worth understanding how a rose grows and flowers before you prune.

Look at the rose: you'll see that flowers are produced either from side shoots growing from the main stems or from new shoots emerging from the base. Both types can be pruned to about 4–5in (10–15cm), around the time that new growth is starting (pp.236–237). This will encourage the plant to produce more side shoots, which will flower the same season. The following winter, these stems can be pruned again in the same way. If the rose is getting too tall, cut the main stems to below the side stems' point of origin.

Also look for any stems that look old—rough and brown in contrast to the smooth, young, green stems. Cut these out: they will probably produce poor-quality flowers, and if you trace them to the top they will often show weak growth. They are also more likely to suffer from disease. Finally, remove any dead, diseased, or otherwise weak-looking stems, along with any remaining leaves. If all of the stems look very old, rejuvenative pruning may be the best option (p.237).

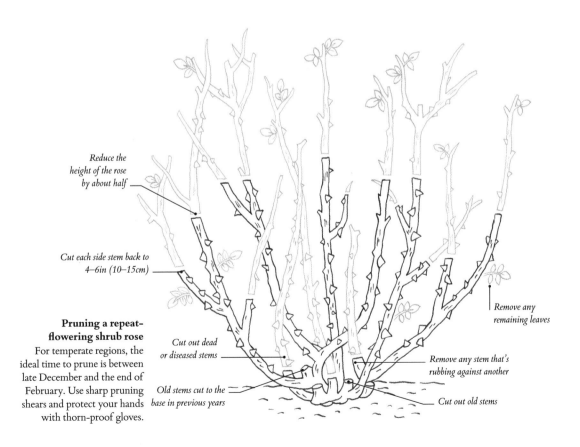

Reduce the height of the rose by about half

Cut each side stem back to 4–6in (10–15cm)

Remove any remaining leaves

Pruning a repeat-flowering shrub rose
For temperate regions, the ideal time to prune is between late December and the end of February. Use sharp pruning shears and protect your hands with thorn-proof gloves.

Cut out dead or diseased stems

Remove any stem that's rubbing against another

Old stems cut to the base in previous years

Cut out old stems

Having finished, step back and assess the plant. Does it look balanced? Is it the shape and size you want? Have all the dead or diseased stems been removed? Make any further tweaks and then remove any leaves remaining on the stems, since they are likely to carry over pests and disease from one season to the next. It's also good to weed around the rose and then mulch the ground beneath it to bury any fallen leaves, which may harbor pests or diseases.

Climbers and ramblers

Far more important than the process of pruning, when it comes to climbers and ramblers, is choosing the right variety in the first place. Try and match the vigor of the rose with the size of the structure or area that you want it to cover. Do not be tempted to choose a variety that will reach the top of the wall or obelisk in one or two seasons, since it will simply continue growing and become a menace.

Any climber or rambler you want to train against a structure such as a fence or an arch (p.238) can be pruned in the same way. In terms of flowering, climbers and ramblers work in a similar way to repeat-flowering shrubs, the only difference being that the flowering side shoots are produced off much longer main stems. Let these main stems grow as long as you need them to be, and shorten the side shoots to about 2–6in (5–15cm), depending on how neat a look is required. If you want to keep the growth tight, reduce them to one or two buds, or around 2in (5cm). Leave them longer for a more informal look. As with shrub roses, once they've been pruned, the side shoots will produce more side shoots which should be pruned in the same way the following winter. This process can continue until the original stem starts looking old and tired, at which stage it should be cut out completely.

When growing up trees, ramblers are effectively inaccessible for pruning and have to be left alone. They will cope perfectly well without any help from pruning shears.

Making the cuts

The general rule, for whatever climate you live in, is to prune roses when new growth is just starting. Any earlier and there is a risk of prematurely encouraging young shoots that will then be susceptible to frost damage. Any later and many young shoots will be lost by cutting or knocking them off, since the roses will be actively growing by then; the first flowers will therefore appear later.

In regions with a temperate climate, sometime between late December and the end of February is ideal. In Mediterranean climates with little frost, pruning can start in late November or early December, but should finish by the end of January. In hot climates, the period of dormancy may well be in midsummer and so the main prune should be done then.

If a rose sends out long shoots toward the end of the year, it's good to cut these back by a third to a half to prevent them from breaking in winter winds and to keep the plant looking reasonably neat.

The only tool you'll need for nearly all pruning tasks is a good pair of sharp pruning shears. If the rose is old, with substantial stems, you'll also need loppers and a pruning saw. Gloves are essential—not so thin that the thorns puncture them, but not so thick that they limit your movement.

Most "rules" about how and where a rose stem should be pruned can be safely ignored. While some will tell you that the stem must be cut at an angle, in fact, this makes no difference. This rule may well have come from the days before pruning shears were invented, when pruning was done with a knife and involved slicing at an angle. Indeed, it is probably better to cut straight across, since it exposes less cut stem. The distance above the bud is not crucial either. While there may be some dieback if a cut is made an inch or so above a bud, it is rarely of any consequence and is soon hidden by leaves. And life is too short to worry about searching for that outward-pointing bud! Better to concentrate on cutting the stem at the right place to create an attractively shaped plant.

Rejuvenating a neglected rose

If a rose hasn't been pruned properly (or, indeed, at all) for a number of years, the stems will have become old and woody and the rose too tall. The simplest way of dealing with this is to cut all the stems hard back to around 1ft (30cm). This can either be done all in one season or, if the rose is looking a bit feeble, stretched out over two. With a bit of luck, new shoots will be produced in spring, seemingly from nowhere, and a beautifully rejuvenated rose will result.

Training a climbing rose on a structure

The simplest support system is rust-proof screws spaced at regular intervals. You need about 1in (2.5cm) to protrude from the wall, so 3in (7.5cm) screws work well. Trellis is another quick and easy option. Stems should be tied on rather than tucked behind, as this may push the trellis away in time and will make cutting older stems out much more difficult. A less conspicuous support is horizontal wires about 18in (50cm) apart, attached to vine eyes to keep them away from the wall. Tensioners should be used to keep the wires taut, and the stems should be tied on to the outside of the wires.

String is the obvious choice for tying the rose stems to their supports, and it should be thick and strong enough that it does not break in windy conditions. Tie loosely, to allow for the stems to grow and get thicker. Hollow, stretchy plastic tubing is a good alternative. Wire should not be used as it will easily cut into the stem.

Stems trained horizontally or diagonally will produce more flowers than vertical shoots, so your goal should be to fan them out to fill the space you have and tie them onto supporting wires or trellis with soft twine.

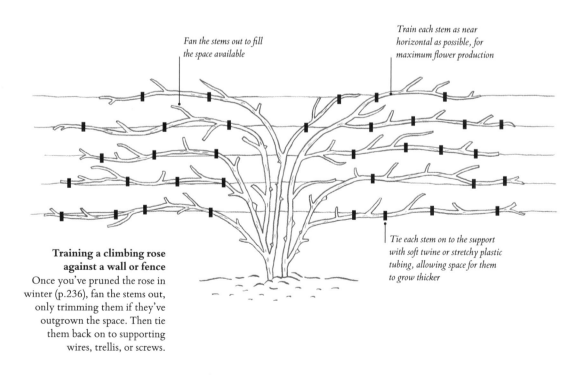

Fan the stems out to fill the space available

Train each stem as near horizontal as possible, for maximum flower production

Tie each stem on to the support with soft twine or stretchy plastic tubing, allowing space for them to grow thicker

Training a climbing rose against a wall or fence
Once you've pruned the rose in winter (p.236), fan the stems out, only trimming them if they've outgrown the space. Then tie them back on to supporting wires, trellis, or screws.

If your rose isn't thriving

Any problem is easiest to remedy if spotted early,
but most can be put right—in the most drastic
cases, by removing it altogether.

Prevention is better than cure

The easiest ways to ensure a rose stays healthy is to choose a naturally disease-resistant variety in the first place, and to prepare the ground well before planting (pp.224–225). It's also a good idea to mix roses with other plants. This makes it more difficult for pests and diseases to move from one rose to the next and encourages beneficial insects that will help reduce pest numbers. Give each rose enough space to ensure good airflow, so that the leaves dry quickly, thereby reducing the incidence of disease. Good pruning, regular mulching, feeding, and watering, if necessary, will also keep your roses in top health.

The lower the level of disease in your garden, the healthier your roses are likely to stay, as there'll be fewer disease spores floating around. If, despite your best efforts, the rose becomes badly diseased and its condition does not improve, replace it with a more naturally disease-resistant one. Make sure to improve the soil first if planning to replant in the same spot (p.225).

Pests and diseases can easily overwinter on roses. The older the stem, the more likely it is to harbor pests and diseases, which is why old stems should be cut out and fresh new ones allowed to replace them when you prune the rose in winter. Stripping off any remaining leaves and burying any fallen ones under a good layer of mulch will also reduce the chance of reinfection in spring. The harder you prune, the more likely you are to remove all sources of infection, although this should be balanced against the risk of overpruning, which may shorten the rose's life.

Spotting symptoms

Keeping a close eye on your roses and diagnosing any problems early on will ensure that any treatments are much more likely to be effective.

The rose's growth is weak

Sometimes a plant just looks sickly: it may be growing slowly, not producing many flowering stems, or not flowering as much as it should.

• **Is it having to compete with other plants?** A mat of plants growing right around the base of the rose is likely to starve it of water and nutrients. Pull them out and keep the space clear under a mulch of organic material. A tree or hedge close by may also be taking advantage of the extra water and nutrients you're giving the rose. Box and yew hedges are especially guilty of this, since their roots tend to be near the surface. These can be cut back or prevented from encroaching by sinking a thick sheet of polyethylene to a depth of about 1ft (30cm).

• **Is it getting enough sun?** Most roses need at least six hours of full sun a day in the growing season, and even the more shade-tolerant varieties (pp.188–193) need four hours. If nearby plants are shading the rose out, cut them back; otherwise, the only option is to transplant the rose in winter to a better spot (p.226).

• **Perhaps the soil is too acid or alkaline?** Roses like it to be just either side of neutral, around pH 6–7.5, and don't appreciate anything too much outside of this range. Soil pH can be easily tested using a home kit, and if it's too acid, you can add lime to remedy the problem. Making an alkaline soil more acidic is more difficult, but it can be done by using sulfur chips.

• **Is the soil it's planted in getting waterlogged or, at the other extreme, draining too fast?** While roses can cope with a wide range of soil types, they do not like extremes of clay or sand. Both can be improved by using generous quantities of well-rotted organic matter, but this needs to be applied before planting. The only option, therefore, is transplanting (p.226). For similar spots where you'd like to plant roses, the varieties recommended for wild areas on pp.136–141 are better choices.

• **Was it planted where another rose was previously growing?** Swapping one rose for another can cause rose replant disease, which stunts growth. If the soil is in a reasonable condition, improve it by applying a generous amount of rotted organic matter and mycorrhizal fungi. If the soil is seriously depleted, you may need to replace the soil entirely (p.225).

If there's no obvious cause, poor growth may be due to an excess or deficiency of a nutrient. To check for this, you will need to send a soil sample away to a lab for analysis. The most common problems are an excess or deficiency of potassium and/or phosphorus. Deficiencies are easily remedied by applying an appropriate fertilizer. An excess is often the result of applying too much fertilizer or animal manure. There is no quick cure for this, as high levels of these nutrients take many years to reduce, during which time moderate amounts of nitrogen only (preferably organic) should be applied. (Excessive nitrogen produces tall stems with little strength and increased susceptibility to pests and diseases.)

Finally, remember that even roses that have been cared for have a finite life span, which depends on the type of rose and the conditions it is growing in. After 15–20 years, many shrub roses will start losing vigor, and you may want to replace them. Climbers, ramblers, repeat- and once-flowering old roses and species roses last longer—sometimes 100 years or more.

It's growing unusual stems

In the UK and much of Europe, nearly all roses are budded onto a rootstock, generally *Rosa laxa* and occasionally *Rosa multiflora*. Elsewhere (particularly North America and Australia), the red climber 'Dr. Huey' and the white rambler *Rosa fortuneana* are used. This is done to encourage strong growth and make a plant of saleable size as quickly as possible. Unfortunately, the rootstock occasionally starts growing alongside the grafted rose and these suckers, if not removed promptly, can completely swamp it. The easiest way to identify *R. laxa* and *R. multiflora* stems is to examine the youngest emerging leaves: if they have any hint of red, the stem is not a sucker. If they are pure green and the number of leaflets, and the shape and quantity of thorns, differ from the rest of the rose, it's a sucker. Dig down so you can pull it off or cut it out where it joins the root.

If the sucker flowers, that usually makes matters clear. *R. laxa* and *R. multiflora* have small, white or pale-pink, single flowers, and *R. fortuneana* has small, double, white flowers. 'Dr. Huey' has bright-red, semi-double flowers. However, if the sucker has reached this stage, it's probably too late to safely remove it completely without damaging the rose beyond repair. The best solution would be to replace the whole plant or else to cut the suckers back regularly.

Standard or tree roses can sometimes sprout very straight, upright shoots coming from the stem. These should be removed as soon as they are spotted.

It's being eaten

It can be frustrating to find the foliage of your roses peppered with holes, or the stems colonized by pests. Whether you need to be concerned about such damage will depend on the pest in question and the severity of its impact.

- **The soft growing tips of new leaves and flower buds are smothered in tiny bugs.** These are aphids: usually ⅛–¼in (3–5mm) long and generally green, but sometimes pink or black. (Their dead remains are white and often confused with white fly.) Probably the most commonly seen pest on roses, aphids suck sap and then excrete honeydew, which is sticky and can cause sooty (black) mold on the leaves below. They are able to increase their numbers at a phenomenal rate, but, luckily, are also a popular source of food for a wide range of insects and birds, so are rarely too much of a problem. As a last resort, severe infestations can be controlled by squashing or knocking them off.

- **If leaves and flowers are being eaten,** this may be caused by the Japanese beetle. These are about 3–4in (8–10mm) long, with coppery-bronze wings and a metallic-green thorax and head. They are prevalent on the East Coast of North America, where they cause damage to many plants, including roses (especially fragrant ones). Control is difficult, as they fly in from some distance away. If spotted, knock into a bucket of soapy water; ideally, do this early in the morning, before they attract others with their pheremones.

- **Distorted flowers (or none at all)** may indicate the presence of the rose midge, which is almost impossible to see with the naked eye. The adults lay their eggs on young shoots, which are then eaten by the developing larvae, leading to poor flower development. By the time the damage is noticeable, it's too late: the larvae will have pupated and fallen to the ground. Almost impossible to control; remove affected buds and flowers.

- **Distorted or heavily marked flowers** can result from flower thrips feeding on the petals. The brown markings look worst on white or pale-colored blooms. Flower thrips are tiny, barely visible to the naked eye, and difficult (if not impossible) to control, although are less of a problem in cool climates. Remove affected buds and flowers where necessary.

- **Missing buds, young shoots, or whole leaves** will be the work of rabbits, hares, or deer, which are all very fond of rose-related food. The classic symptom of rabbit and hare damage is the absence of leaflets, with just the leaf stalk remaining, as well as scratchings in the soil and droppings. Deer damage is often more severe and frustrating, as they will take the flower buds. There are sprays that can be applied that will deter these herbivores, but they need to be reapplied on a regular basis and also switched around, since the deer may get used to the smell. The only permanent

Aphids

Japanese beetle

Rose midge

Flower thrip

Hormonal weedkiller damage

Chili thrips

Rose rosette virus

Black spot

prevention is to erect a suitable fence. A possible, much cheaper, alternative is to stretch four or five strands of strong fishing line spaced 1ft (30cm) apart: the deer will not see them and will hopefully shy away and look elsewhere for something to eat. You could also try planting *Rosa rugosa* and its hybrids, whose very thorny stems may be unpalatable to these browsers.

The leaves are distorted

• **Smaller, narrower leaves** indicate damage caused by hormonal herbicide, such as glyphosate and selective weed killers applied to lawns. They shouldn't be used at all in the garden, but if you absolutely must, keep them far away from your roses, and avoid applying them when the wind is blowing in their direction. Depending on the dosage, the rose may not survive.

• **Distorted leaves and stems** may be a sign of chili thrips, which are known to be spreading throughout North America. Like flower thrips (see opposite), they are barely visible to the naked eye and almost impossible to control; the best course of action is to remove infected buds and flowers.

• **Excessively branched, thorny red stems** (that don't green up over time) indicate rose rosette virus. It is spread by a wingless, wind-spread mite and thus impossible to control, while causing a great deal of damage. There is no cure: the whole rose should be dug up and disposed of as soon as possible.

There are marks on the leaves or stems

There are a number of diseases that cause these symptoms, and they can be tricky to tell apart.

• **Black or charcoal-gray circular spots** on the upper side of the leaf only, ¼–½in (5–10mm) across with a soft edge, or sometimes lines radiating out of them, are caused by black spot—probably the most common of all rose diseases. If the attack is bad, the spots coalesce and the leaves turn yellow between the spots, before dropping off. In severe attacks, the rose loses all its leaves, which weakens it and looks very unattractive. Leaves staying wet for long periods encourages black spot, which is why it's important to water roses during the day rather than too early or late. Susceptibility is highly variable— some varieties are completely resistant, while others are extremely prone. The great majority will get some, and it can be tolerated if not too severe. Apply a foliar feed (seaweed-based, for instance) as soon as you spot the first sign of black spot. (Even better: apply this regularly from the start of the growing season, especially if you know a rose is susceptible). Make sure you give any more vulnerable roses the best possible growing conditions. Only remove leaves if they're badly affected. Removing those that are still partly green will reduce the plant's ability to photosynthesize and so potentially weaken it. Two or three applications of a suitable fungicide may also help.

• **Dark (often dark purple), irregularly shaped areas** indicate downy mildew. They tend to have a sharp edge and are commonly bounded by the leaf veins, on the upper side of the leaf. This often causes severe leaf drop, which in some very susceptible varieties can occur when the dark areas are hardly noticeable. Spots are sometimes also seen on the stems, when they are quite small and more distinctly purple. Downy mildew is particularly prevalent in times of high humidity and when the leaves are wet for long periods, especially in spring and again in the fall. Again, try to minimize the length of time the leaves are wet by watering during the warmth of the day. Susceptibility varies according to the variety, although miniatures and a number of ramblers are more susceptible.

Downy mildew

• **Small, dark spots** up to ¼in (5mm) across, developing into rings with gray centers, are a sign of either *Anthracnose* or *Cercospora* fungi. Neither usually cause too much harm. As with black spot and downy mildew, some varieties of rose are prone to infections, and the likelihood of them occurring is increased by the leaves being wet for prolonged periods.

Cercospora

• **White powdery deposits** on leaves and young stems are caused by powdery mildew, which sometimes also causes distortion of the young leaves. It is very variety-specific, some of the wichurana ramblers like 'Dorothy Perkins' being especially susceptible to it. Dryness at the roots or leaves being wet for long periods make it more likely. Paradoxically, wetting the leaves can help to reduce it: the presence of water prevents the spores from germinating. You must do this around the middle of the day, though, when it's windy and sunny, so they dry out quickly.

Powdery mildew

• **Small yellow spots** on the upper side of the leaf, corresponding with orange pustules on the underside, are a sign of rust. The orange on the underside turns black later in the season. This can cause severe leaf drop and a general reduction in vigor. Resistance is very variable from variety to variety and since it is difficult to control by cultural methods it is particularly important to choose resistant varieties.

Rust

• **Mottled leaves,** with no marks visible underneath, are likely the work of leaf hoppers. These green bugs, around ¼in (5mm) long, often fly or hop away when disturbed. They suck the sap, but are rarely serious and can be ignored.

However, if tiny, insectlike creatures can be seen on the underside of leaves, with mottling and spotting on the upper side, this indicates red spider-mite infection. Almost invisible to the naked eye, the mites suck sap from the underside of leaves, weakening the plant. If left unchecked, they

Leaf hopper mottling

Leaf hoppers

Red spider mite

Chlorosis

Rose mosaic virsus

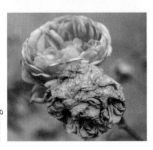

Balling

eventually form a weblike covering over the top of the shoot. Red spider mites are sometimes seen in mild climates, but are more common in hot, dry climates where they can cause serious damage. Regular sprays of water on the underside of the leaves may help to control them.

• **Leaves turning pale**, known as chlorosis, is a symptom that suggests the rose is suffering from a nutrient deficiency, or soil the pH being too high or low. A lab test will pinpoint the cause, most often an excess or deficiency of potassium, phosphorus, or magnesium, which can be remedied by applying an appropriate fertilizer (p.241).

• **An irregular pattern of yellow patches and lines** on the upper side of the leaf is usually a sign of rose mosaic virus. The symptoms are very variable. There are no known vectors, nor do pruning shears spread it. It is only known to have been passed from one plant to the next by budding or grafting. While it doesn't look good, it rarely causes much harm.

The flowers won't open

This is known as "balling." It happens in wet weather, soft-petaled varieties with many petals being more susceptible to it. You may be able to save the flower by pulling off the confining outer petals, so releasing the inner ones. Once the weather has improved, new flowers will open normally.

The best remedies

We all want a magic answer when a favorite plant is attacked, but I advocate that patience and good gardening methods are the best long-term solutions to any problems your roses have. The best approach is a natural, organic one: follow the suggestions on p.239, and take good care of your soil and all the plants in your garden. A liquid foliar feed (seaweed, garlic, or similar), applied regularly even before any problems are visible, may be the best medicine for most diseases. It's difficult to produce perfectly pest- and disease-free roses; better to accept and live with low levels, and know that in the case of pests, they're supplying food for the other wildlife in your garden.

Chemical controls should be considered a last resort. In some countries, fungicides and pesticides are available for controlling specific problems, but need to be used with care, as they can harm the environment. Fungicides against black spot and mildew should be used as a preventative, and pesticides only when the chances of harming any other insects is nonexistent. Always use them on a windless day, so you can control where they land, and take care to protect yourself and your pets from any contact with them.

Glossary

Annual
A plant that completes its life cycle, from germination to flowering, seeding, and then death, in one growing season.

Bare-root
A nursery-grown plant sold with no soil or container. Usually sold in winter, when the plant is dormant.

Budding
See grafting.

Containerized
A nursery-grown plant sold in a container with compost.

Cross-pollination
When pollen from one plant fertilizes the flower of another, producing a hybrid variety.

Cutting
A section of a plant that is removed and used for propagation (p.228).

Dead-head
To remove spent flower heads in order to promote further growth or flowering, or to improve the plant's appearance.

Double flower
A form of flower with at least 30 petals, and with the stamens absent or not visible (at least initially).

Fully double flower
A form of flower with at least 60 petals, often giving a rosette appearance, and with the stamens absent or or obscured, even when the bloom is fully open.

Grafting
A technique used by commercial growers, by which an artificial union is made between two plants. The bud of the desired plant is grafted on to the rootstock of another, in order to encourage strong growth and produce a large plant quickly (p.228).

Hardiness
How resistant a plant is to cold. Hardiness rating systems differ between countries; for example, in the US, USDA zones are used, while in the UK, the RHS uses "H" numbers.

Hardy
Plants that are able to withstand outdoor conditions year-round, including temperatures below freezing, without protection.

Hips
The fruit of a rose plant, which contains the rose's seed. Typically produced in the fall, the brightly colored hips can provide both late-season interest and a source of food for birds.

Layering
A method of propagation in which a stem is induced to root by being pegged down into the soil, while still attached to the parent plant (p.228).

Mulch
A layer of organic material, such as manure, compost, or wood chips, applied to the top of soil in order to help retain moisture, suppress weeds, and protect and feed the soil.

NPK
Short for "nitrogen, phosphorus, potassium," the nutritional breakdown of fertilizer, typically expressed as a ratio (e.g., 5:5:10).

Perennial
A plant that lives for at least three seasons. Also known as "herbaceous perennials," they die down at the end of each growing season.

pH
The level of acidity or alkalinity of soil or compost depicted on a scale from 1 to 14, which can be assessed using a testing kit (p.208). Roses need soil to be close to neutral (pH7), typically in the 6–7.5 range.

Rejuvenate
To cut all stems back hard to near ground level, in order to encourage new shoots to grow from the base. Normally done to a rose that has not been pruned properly for a number of years.

Root ball
The roots and accompanying soil or compost visible when a plant is lifted.

Rootstock
A plant used to provide the root system for a grafted (budded) plant.

Semi-double flower
A form of flower with more petals than a single flower (usually eight to 14).

Single flower
A form of flower with one row of usually five to seven petals, or as few as four in exceptional cases.

Species rose
A naturally occuring type; also known as a wild rose (p.64).

Specimen
A plant with a striking shape that looks good on its own or as a centerpiece of a larger display.

Standard
A shrub grafted on to a rootstock with a clear length of stem below the graft, lifting the rose up to make a treelike shape.

Sucker
A shoot that arises from below ground level directly from the roots. Grafted (budded) roses may occasionally produce suckers from the rootstock, which need to be removed (p.241).

Training
A method of guiding the direction of a plant's growth by arranging and securing its stems, in order to encourage more flowers and better coverage of a surface.

Tender
A plant that is sensitive to frost.

Resources

Organizations and resources

For more information about specific rose varieties, find a local rose society, or to become involved with rose conservation, take a look at these organizations and resources.

American Rose Society
rose.org

Canadian Rose Society
canadianrosesociety.org

Royal Horticultural Society
www.rhs.org.uk

Combined Rose List:
The International Rose Directory (updated annually)
www.combinedroselist.com

Help Me Find
helpmefind.com/rose/plants

Heritage Rose Society
heritagerosefoundation.org

Historic Roses Group
historicroses.org

World Federation of Rose Societies
www.worldrose.org

US and Canadian nurseries and suppliers

A reputable supplier is a must when sourcing roses for your garden. I recommend looking into the following nurseries as a starting point for your search.

David Austin Roses
davidaustinroses.com

Spring Hill Nurseries (Ohio)
springhillnursery.com

High Country Roses (Colorado)
highcountryroses.com

Chamblee's Rose Nursery (Texas)
chambleeroses.com

Regan Nursery (California)
regannursery.com

Roses Unlimited (South Carolina)
rosesunlimitedsc.com

Antique Rose Emporium (Texas)
antiqueroseemporium.com

Otto & Sons (California)
ottoandsonsnursery.com

Weeks Roses (California)
weeksroses.com

Corn Hill Nursery
(New Brunswick, Canada)
cornhillnursery.com

Rogue Valley Roses (Oregon)
roguevalleyroses.com

Heirloom Roses (Oregon)
heirloomroses.com

Palatine Roses (Ontario, Canada)
palatineroses.com

Garden Crossings (Michigan)
gardencrossings.com

Northland Rosarium (Washington)
northlandrosarium.com

Angel Garden (Florida)
www.angelgardens.com

Recommended further reading

Book of Perennials, Claire Austin
(White Hopton Publications,
2020)

The English Roses, David Austin
(ACC Art Books, 2021)

The English Roses, David Austin
(Conran Octopus 2017)

The Rose, David Austin
(Garden Art Press, 2013)

Tea Roses, Lynn Chapman, Et al.
(Rosenberg Publishing, 2008)

Rosor för nordiska trädgårdar,
Lars-Åke Gustavsson
(Natur och Kultur 1999)

Compendium of Rose Diseases,
R. Kenneth Horst (American
Phytopathological Society, 2007)

Rosa: The Story of the Rose, Peter
Kukielski with Charles Philips
(Yale University Press, 2021)

Roses Without Chemicals, Peter
Kukielski (Timber Press, 2015)

The Gardener's Book of Colour,
Andrew Lawson (Pimpernel
Press, 2015)

*By Any Other Name: A Cultural
History of the Rose*, Simon Morley
(Oneworld, 2021)

The Ultimate Guide to Roses,
Roger Phillips and Martyn Rix
(Macmillan, 2004)

The Rose, Jennifer Potter (Atlantic
Books, 2011)

RHS Encyclopaedia of Roses,
Charles Quest-Ritson and Brigid
Quest-Ritson (DK, 2008)

The Rose Doctor, Gary Ritchie
(2019)

Encyclopedia of Rose Science,
ed. Dr. Andrew Roberts

The English Flower Garden, William
Robinson (Bloomsbury, 1998)

The History of the Rose in Denmark,
Torben Thim (Centifolia, 2018)

*The Graham Stuart Thomas Rose
Book* (John Murray, 1994)

Everyday Roses, Paul Zimmerman
(Taunton Press, 2013)

Roses in Bermuda, Bermuda Rose
Society Book Committee (2013)

Index

Page numbers in *italics*
refer to illustrations

Acknowledgments

Author acknowledgments

My thanks to Chris Young for suggesting that I should write this book and then to my partner, Rosie Irving, who, despite my hesitation, persuaded me that it would be a good idea and then for her continued positivity.

Also to the DK team for bringing the book together so beautifully. They include Ruth O'Rourke, Amy Slack, Jane Birdsell, Emily Hedges, Vicky Read, and Glenda Fisher.

For getting me into the world of roses, I owe a huge amount of thanks to the late David Austin, who, despite my very limited knowledge at the time, took me on as nursery manager.

In the rose world, there are many to thank with whom I have discussed roses in all their great diversity. They include Richard Stubbs and Stephen Parnham of David Austin Roses, Thomas Proll of Kordes Roses, John Anthony, chairman of the Rose Society UK, Charles and Brigid Quest-Ritson, and Paul Zimmerman of Paul Zimmerman Roses.

Publisher acknowledgments

For their help in sourcing and providing images for the book, DK would like to thank Howard Rice, Eriko Nakakawaji, Thomas Proll (Kordes Roses), Stephen Parnham, and Paul Zimmerman. Thanks also to Francesco Piscitelli for proofreading, Vanessa Bird for indexing, and Vagisha Pushp for preparing picture credits.

Picture credits
The publisher would like to thank the following for their kind permission to reproduce their photographs:

(Key: **a**-above; **b**-below/bottom; **c**-centre; **f**-far; **l**-left; **r**-right; **t**-top)

2-3 Clive Nichols: Wynyard Hall, County Durham. **9 Bridgeman Images**. **10 Bridgeman Images**: © Fitzwilliam Museum). **13 Alamy Stock Photo**: Artepics. **15 Bridgeman Images**: by courtesy of Julian Hartnoll. **19 Howard Rice**: The David Austin Rose Gardens, Shropshire, UK. **20-21 Clive Nichols**: Glyndebourne, East Sussex. The Mary Christie Rose Garden. **22 Howard Rice**: Hatton Grange, Shropshire, UK. **25 Clive Nichols**: André Eve Garden, France. **26 Yokohama English Garden**: Y. Sakurano. **28 Clive Nichols**: Manor Farm, Cheshire. **30 Marianne Majerus**. **31 Howard Rice**. **32 Clive Nichols**. **34 © Andrea Jones/Garden Exposures Photo Library**. **35 Jonathan Buckley**. **37 © Andrea Jones/Garden Exposures Photo Library**. **38-39 Hervé Lenain**: Les Jardins de Roquelin. **40 Alamy Stock Photo**: Michael Wheatley Photography. **41 Marianne Majerus**: Design: Rupert Wheeler and Paul Gazerwitz. **43 Yokohama English Garden**: Y. Sakurano. **44 Carolyn Parker**. **46 © Andrea Jones/Garden Exposures Photo Library**. **47 Clive Nichols**: Ellicar Gardens, near Doncaster. **50 © Andrea Jones/Garden Exposures Photo Library**. **51 Rachel Warne**: Design Jo Thompson. **53 Howard Rice**. **54-55 Clive Nichols**: Rockcliffe Garden, Gloucestershire. **57 Alamy Stock Photo**: Lioneska. **58 © Andrea Jones/Garden Exposures Photo Library**. **59 GAP Photos**. **62 bl GAP Photos**: Howard Rice / Cambridge University Botanic Gardens; **bc GAP Photos**: Jonathan Buckley; **br GAP Photos**: Nova Photo Graphik. **63 Clive Nichols**: Mottisfont Abbey, Hampshire. **64 bl GAP Photos**: Michael Howes. **64 cl GAP Photos**: Ian Thwaites. **65 Howard Rice**. **66 GAP Photos**: Carole Drake / Garden: Westbrook House, Somerset; Owners and Designers: Keith Anderson and David Mendel. **67 GAP Photos**: Nicola Stocken. **68 GAP Photos**: Christa Brand. **69 GAP Photos**: Keith Burdett. **70 cl GAP Photos**: Howard Rice, **b** Jonathan Buckley. **71 Jonathan Buckley**. **72 Howard Rice**. **73 Marianne Majerus**: Design Rachel Bebb. **74 tl GAP Photos**: Christina Bollen; **cl GAP Photos**: Howard Rice. **75 cr GAP Photos**: Howard Rice; **br GAP Photos**: Richard Bloom. **76 David Austin Roses**. **77 Marianne Majerus**: Design: Acres Wild. **78 Marianne Majerus**. **79 GAP Photos**: Howard Rice. **80 Marianne Majerus**: Rymans, Sussex. **81 GAP Photos**: Howard Rice / Location: The Manor House, Stevington. **82 John Glover**. **83 Marianne Majerus**: Design: Dominick Murphy, Ireland. **84 cl GAP Photos**: Howard Rice; **bl © Andrea Jones/Garden Exposures Photo Library**. **85 © Andrea Jones/Garden Exposures Photo Library**. **89 Rachel Warne**: Design: Jo Thompson. **90 GAP Photos**: Evgeniya Vlasova. **91 GAP Photos**: Howard Rice. **92 t GAP Photos**: FhF Greenmedia; **b Alamy Stock Photo**: Lindsay Constable. **93 tr David Austin Roses**; **93 br Bailey Nurseries**. **95 tl Bailey Nurseries**; **bl GAP Photos**: Nova Photo Graphik; **br GAP Photos**: Visions. **96 Howard Rice**. **97 t GAP Photos**: Howard Rice; **b Alamy Stock Photo**: Avalon.red / Photos Horticultural. **98 Star® Roses and Plants**. **99t Star® Roses and Plants**; **b Kordes Roses**. **101 tl GAP Photos**: Howard Rice / David Austin Roses; **tr Clive Nichols**: André Eve Rose Nursery, France; **bl GAP Photos**: J S Sira; **br David Austin Roses**. **102 Star® Roses and Plants**. **103 t GAP Photos**: Carole Drake - Garden: Westbrook House, Somerset; Owners and Designers: Keith Anderson and David Mendel; **b GAP Photos**: Howard Rice. **104 tl Star® Roses and Plants**; **tr Kordes Roses**. **105 tl Marianne Majerus**; **tc Getty Images / iStock**: / schnuddel; **tr ©Meilland International**. **106-107 Marianne Majerus Garden Images**: Design: Acres Wild.

107 br David Austin Roses. 108 GAP Photos: Joanna Kossak / Designer: Claudia de Yong. 109 t Star® Roses and Plants; br. GAP Photos: Dave Zubraski. 110 t GAP Photos: Richard Bloom; bl Botanikfoto: / Steffen Hauser. 111 GAP Photos: Rob Whitworth ; b GAP Photos: Jonathan Buckley. 112 tl GAP Photos: Doreen Wynja; tc Jackson & Perkins; tr ©Meilland International. 113 tl GAP Photos: Jo Whitworth; tc David Austin Roses; tr GAP Photos: Jenny Lilly. 114 l GAP Photos: Richard Wareham. 114–115 Clive Nichols: Wynyard Hall, County Durham. 115 r Alamy Stock Photo: Matthew Taylor. 117 tl and br Kordes Roses; tr and bl © Andres Jones/Garden Exposures Photo Library. 118 GAP Photos: Jonathan Buckley. 119 GAP Photos: Howard Rice. 120 l Kordes Roses; r GAP Photos: Doreen Wynja. 121 l Kordes Roses; c © Andrea Jones Garden Exposures Photo Library; r Star® Roses and Plants. 122 t Kordes Roses; r David Austin Roses. 123 GAP Photos: Howard Rice. 124 Kordes Roses. 125 t Harkness Roses; b Star® Roses and Plants. 127 tl David Austin Roses; tr, bl and br Kordes Roses. 128 t Kordes Roses; b Weeks Roses; 129 Star® Roses and Plants. 130 l GAP Photos: Howard Rice; r Saxon Holt. 131 Kordes Roses. 133 tl GAP Photos: Julie Dansereau; tr Howard Rice; bl GAP Photos: Jacqui Dracup; br Kordes Roses. 134 l Kordes Roses. 134–135 GAP Photos: Robert Mabic. 135 r GAP Photos: Jonathan Need. 136 Botanikfoto: Hans-Roland Mülle. 137 Shutterstock. com: mcajan. 139 tl GAP Photos: Pernilla Bergdahl; tr GAP Photo: Mark Bolton; bl GAP Photo: Howard Rice; br Alamy Stock Photo: Sharon Talson. 140 t Alamy Stock Photo: Garden Photo World /David C Phillips; b Marianne Majerus. 141 t GAP Photos: Matteo Carassale; b GAP Photos: Zara Napier. 142 t GAP Photos: Nicola Stocken; b GAP Photo: Howard Rice. 143 t GAP Photos: Jonathan Buckley; b Howard Rice. 144 tl Weeks Roses; tc GAP Photos: Ellen Rooney; tr GAP Photos:John Glover. 145 l GAP Photos: Nicola Stocken; c David Austin Roses; tr Star® Roses and Plants. 146 t GAP Photos: Rob Whitworth, b Marianne Majerus Garden Images: Design: Acres Wild. 147 t GAP Photos: Martin Hughes-Jones; b GAP Photos: Annie Green-Armytage. 148–149 Marianne Majerus Garden Images: Design: Acres Wild. 149 br GAP Photos: Sabina Ruber. 151 t Alamy Stock Photo: Imagebroker; tr GAP Photos: Doreen Wynja; bl GAP Photos: Howard Rice; 151 br Shutterstock.com: Sergey V Kalyakin. 152 GAP Photos: Howard Rice. 153 t GAP Photos: Lynn Keddie; b Alamy Stock Photo: Sergey Kalyakin. 154 l Harkness Roses; r GAP Photos: Doreen Wynja. 155 tl Dreamstime.com: André Muller; tc Kordes Roses; tr Star® Roses and Plants. 156–157 GAP Photos: Jonathan Buckley / David Austin Roses. 157 r David Austin Roses; 158 t Lens Roses; b Stephen Parnham. 159 GAP Photos: Howard Rice. 160 t Marianne Majerus; b Botanikfoto: Hans Roland Mülle 161 t Week Roses; b GAP Photos: Martin Hughes-Jones. 162 t Michael Marriott; b GAP Photos: Jonathan Buckley. 163 © Andrea Jones Garden Exposures Photo Library. 164 Kordes Roses. 165 GAP Photos: Howard Rice / Wynyard Hall Rose Garden, Stockton-on-Tees. 166 l Star® Roses and Plants; c Heirloom Roses; r GAP Photos: Nova Photo Graphik. 167 l Alamy Stock Photo: P Tomlins; c Jason Ingram; r GAP Photos: Howard Rice. 168 Shutterstock.com: Clickmanis. 168–169 Howard Rice. 170 GAP Photos: Martin Hughes-Jones. 171 t GAP Photos: Maddie Thornhill; b GAP Photos: Nicola Stocken. 172 bl ©Meilland International. 172–173 Marianne Majerus. 174 l GAP Photos: Dave Zubraski; r Alamy Stock Photo: Jane Tregelles. 175 l Alamy Stock Photo: Organica; c Alamy Stock Photo: Matteo Omied; r GAP Photos: Nova Photo Graphik. 176 t GAP Photos: Benedikt Dittli; b GAP Photos: John Glover. 177 Saxon Holt. 178 l The Bermuda Rose Society. 178–179 Howard Rice. 179 br Himeno Rose Nursery. 181 tl GAP Photos: Maxine

Adcock; tr Malcolm Manners; bl and br Antique Rose Emporium. 182 t GAP Photos: Howard Rice; b Kordes Roses. 183 t GAP Photos: Howard Rice; b Alamy Stock Photo. 184–185 Marianne Majerus: Design: Acres Wild. 185 r Saxon Holt. 186 t GAP Photos: FhF Greenmedia; b Carolyn Parker. 187 t Marianne Majerus; b Paul Zimmerman. 188 GAP Photos: Nicola Stocken. 189 David Austin Roses. 190 t GAP Photos: Heather Edwards; b David Austin. 191 t GAP Photos: Christa Brand; b GAP Photos: Jerry Pavia. 193 tl GAP Photos: Visions; tr and br GAP Photos: Ron Evans; bl GAP Photos:Tim Gainey. 194 t GAP Photos: Leigh Clapp; b GAP Photos: Pernilla Bergdahl. 195 t GAP Photos: Nova Photo Graphik; b GAP Photos: Howard Rice. 196 l and c GAP Photos: Howard Rice; r GAP Photos: Michael Howes. 197 l, c and r GAP Photos: Nova Photo Graphik. 198 GAP Photos: Carole Drake - Garden: Westbrook House, Somerset; Owners and Designers: Keith Anderson and David Mendel. 199 t GAP Photos: Ernie Janes; b GAP Photos: Martin Hughes-Jones. 200 l Star® Roses and Plants. 200–201 Jonathan Buckley. 201 r Shutterstock.com: InfoFlowersPlants. 202 tl GAP Photos; tc Kordes Roses; tr GAP Photos: Howard Rice. 203 tl GAP Photos: Tommy Tonsberg; tc GAP Photos: Martin Hughes-Jones; tr GAP Photos: Nicola Stocken. 204 t GAP Photos: Visions; br GAP Photos: Nova Photo Graphik. 205 b Star® Roses and Plants. 207 t GAP Photos: Lynn Keddie; tr Star® Roses and Plants; bl Kordes Roses; br Howard Rice. 208 ©Pépinières et Roseraies Georges Delbard. 209 t © Meilland International; b GAP Photos: Howard Rice. 210 tl Jason Ingram; tr David Austin Roses. 211 l and c Shutterstock.com: Sergey V Kalyakin; r GAP Photos: Jenny Lilly. 212–213 Marianne Majerus. 213 r GAP Photos. 214 GAP Photos: Howard Rice / David Austin Rose Gardens, Shropshire. 215 t GAP Photos: Jonathan Buckley / David Austin Roses; b GAP Photos: Howard Rice. 216 tl GAP Photos: Annie Green-Armytage; tr GAP Photos: Howard Rice. 217 bl Alamy Stock Photo: Imagebroker; br Himeno Rose Nursery. 218 t GAP Photos: Rob Whitworth; b GAP Photos: Howard Rice. 219 GAP Photos: Paul Debois. 242 Professor Stefan Buczacki: crb, cra. Minden Pictures: crb. naturepl.com: Nigel Cattlin br. 243 Professor Stefan Buczacki: bl. Kordes Roses: tl. Star Roses: clb. 244 Professor Stefan Buczacki: cr. GAP Photos: Geoff Kidd crb. Getty Images / iStock: Natalya Vilman br. Kordes Roses: cra, tr. 245 Kordes Roses: tl. naturepl.com: Nigel Cattlin cla. Howard Rice: bl, cl

Cover images: Front: GAP Photos: Joanna Kossak / Designer: Claudia de Yong; Back: Howard Rice

All other images © Dorling Kindersley

DK | Penguin Random House

Project Editor Amy Slack
Senior Designer Glenda Fisher
Editor Jane Birdsell
Designer Vicky Read
Picture Researcher Emily Hedges
Illustrator Vicky Read
US Editor Margaret Parrish
Production Editor David Almond
Production Controller Rebecca Parton
Jacket Designer Maxine Pedliham
Jacket Editor Jasmin Lennie
Managing Editor Ruth O'Rourke
Managing Art Editor Marianne Markham
Consultant Gardening Publisher Chris Young
Art Director Maxine Pedliham
Publisher Katie Cowan

First American Edition, 2022
Published in the United States by DK Publishing
1450 Broadway, Suite 801, New York, NY 10018

Copyright © 2022 Dorling Kindersley Limited
DK, a Division of Penguin Random House LLC
22 23 24 25 26   10 9 8 7 6 5 4 3 2 1
001-327515-May/2022

A catalog record for this book is available from the Library of Congress.
ISBN 978-0-7440-5681-5

DK books are available at special discounts when purchased
in bulk for sales promotions, premiums, fund-raising, or educational use.
For details, contact: DK Publishing Special Markets,
1450 Broadway, Suite 801, New York, NY 10018
SpecialSales@dk.com

Printed and bound in China

For the curious
www.dk.com

MIX
Paper from
responsible sources
FSC™ C018179

This book was made with Forest Stewardship Council
™ certified paper—one small step in DK's commitment
to a sustainable future. For more information go to
www.dk.com/our-green-pledge.

About the author

From a very young age, Michael Marriott has been a keen gardener, but it wasn't until he joined David Austin Roses in the mid-eighties that he became immersed in the world of roses. As an integral member of the nursery, he played an important role in the popularisation of the English Roses. He is passionate about roses in all their diversity, both as a central plant for the garden and as an important part of so many cultures around the world.

Michael has designed many thousands of rose gardens and borders around the world – private and public, large and small – including the Royal Botanic Gardens Kew, Queen Mary's Rose Garden in Regent's Park, Hampton Court Palace, Wynyard Hall, Trentham Gardens, the David Austin rose garden near Osaka, Japan and even a garden in Bhutan to celebrate the marriage of their King and Queen.

Michael frequently lectures, leads garden tours, and runs workshops both at home and abroad on all aspects of roses as well as writing for magazines. In 2020, he revised and updated David Austin's *The English Roses* (ACC Art Books).

At home, Michael and his partner, Rosie Irving, garden very much along organic lines at home, and this is something he is keen to pass onto anyone with roses in their garden.